"In a time of fear, stress, and polarization, will Christian school leaders try to hunker down behind shrinking tribal boundaries or find transformative ways forward? This book offers hope for the latter. It offers valuable, practical help for those who still envision a thriving future for Christian education."

—David Smith
Director, Kuyers Institute for Christian Teaching and Learning;
Coordinator, de Vries Institute for Global Faculty Development; and
Professor of Education, Calvin University

"This is a hopeful book. The case studies are rigorously researched, accessible to read, and will inspire your school community to feel excited about Christian education for our present times. With Swaner, Eckert, Ellefsen, and Lee, you are in the safest of hands. . . . I am grateful for the way their work is leading and shaping the future of Christian education."

—Beth Green
Provost and Chief Academic Officer, Tyndale University

"Through thorough research and detailed accounts of eleven Christian schools and networks, Swaner, Eckert, Ellefsen, and Lee offer wisdom for navigating recurrent challenges that school leaders face. Speaking as a school board member, these accounts inspire my own redemptive imagination and reassure me of God's faithfulness. . . ."

—Albert Cheng
Professor of Education Policy, University of Arkansas and
Governing Board Member, Anthem Classical Academy

"*Future Ready* offers research-based strategies and real-world examples of innovative programs that challenge us to make our schools more relevant and sustainable for the future while staying true to our mission. I was inspired by this book, and I plan to give a copy to each member of my board and leadership team."

—Julie Ambler
Head of School, The Woodlands Christian Academy and Executive Committee
Vice C͏   ͏rds and Accountability

"Christian schools are developing novel, creative business strategies that can serve as a guiding beacon to all. *Future Ready* gathers top minds in Christian school research to unpack these innovations, drawing out themes and ideas that can assist all leaders in designing new models for their own schools' future viability."

—Jay Ferguson
Head of School, Grace Community School and
Board Chair, Association of Christian Schools International

"The chapters in *Future Ready* cover vital issues around mission and practice. Christian school leaders looking to found, lead, or strengthen Christian schools—whether in conventional models, or in hybrid, micro, or online settings—will find this research invaluable."

—Eric Wearne
Director, National Hybrid Schools Project, Kennesaw State University

"Before the COVID-19 pandemic, only five percent of schools were future-ready. Now every school has no choice but to become future-ready or die. *Future Ready* provides the first roadmap for Christian educators to cross the chasm from the limitations of the past to a hopeful future."

—Rex Miller
Futurist, Author, and MindShift Founder

"Candid, relevant, and timely, *Future Ready* brings a hopeful challenge to Christian schools. Through stories of innovation, change, and cooperation, Christian educators are inspired to be creative, imaginative, and curious about what is possible. . . . The shared experiences found in *Future Ready* spur schools and their leaders to put their faith and their mission into action."

—Jennifer Thompson
Chief Operating Officer, Christian Schools International

FUTURE READY

FUTURE READY

Innovative Missions and Models in Christian Education

Lynn E. Swaner, Jon Eckert,
Erik Ellefsen, and Matthew H. Lee

The Association of Christian Schools International, Colorado Springs, www.acsi.org

Cardus, Hamilton, www.cardus.ca

Scripture quotations marked (NIV) are taken from the Holy Bible, New International Version®, NIV®. Copyright © 1973, 1978, 1984, 2011 by Biblica, Inc.™ Used by permission of Zondervan. All rights reserved worldwide. www.zondervan.com

The "NIV" and "New International Version" are trademarks registered in the United States Patent and Trademark Office by Biblica, Inc.™

Published 2022

Printed in the United States of America

28 27 26 25 24 23 22   1 2 3 4 5 6 7

Future Ready: Innovative Missions and Models in Christian Education

ISBN-13: 978-1-58331-223-0 (paper)

ISBN-13: 978-1-58331-224-7 (e-book)

Copyedited by Jeff Reimer
Cover image by iStock.com/phototechno
Designed by Alicia Vanderwillik and Domenic Sallese
Edited by Lisa Richmond and Lynn E. Swaner, with the assistance of Jenisa Los
Photos provided to ACSI by the participating schools

CONTENTS

PREFACE

The authors of this book are old enough to remember what it was like to travel long distances by car before GPS, with our glove boxes filled with printed maps picked up from gas stations along the way. Today, we can all plug a destination into our phone's map app, hit start, and we'll get the correct directions turn by turn. Except when we don't, of course. Sometimes because of a poor signal, new construction, or even a wrong turn we've made, the dreaded "recalculating" message emanates from our phones. We've all been there—praying that a new route appears quickly while we continue to drive without the guidance we've become so dependent on, often at high speeds, and flying by exits we don't know whether we should have taken.

This moment of anxiety has become the norm for many of today's educational leaders, when they think about the direction of their schools, career, and profession. School leadership is perhaps more challenging now than at any previous time in history, filled with both known and unknown obstacles—as well as opportunities. For Christian schools, the world of the last half of the twentieth century, when most of them were founded, no longer exists. It is not surprising that the financial and educational models that Christian schools were built on are often no longer suited to the cultural, social, and market realities of today. Whether we like it or not, this is a "recalculating" moment in Christian education. It's time to move into new places that our trusted maps likely cannot take us.

Two authors have inspired us to think of the future of Christian schools in terms of maps. First, in *Canoeing the Mountains: Christian Leadership in Uncharted Territory*, Tod Bolsinger of Fuller Theological Seminary recounts the two-year exploratory journey of Meriwether Lewis and William Clark through the Louisiana Purchase as going "off the map and into uncharted territory. . . . What lay before them was nothing like what was behind them. There were no experts, no maps, no 'best practices' and no sure guides who could lead them safely and successfully."[1] Bolsinger makes the case that most challenges facing today's organizations are similar, because they are "adaptive" in nature—meaning they "go beyond the technical solutions of resident experts or best practices, or even the organization's current knowledge. They arise when the world around us has changed but we continue to live on the successes of the past."[2]

Tim Elmore applies similar thinking to the field of education in his book *Marching Off the Map: Inspire Students to Navigate a Brand New World*. In recounting the practice of ancient mapmakers of inserting dragons or serpents into corners of the map where land had yet to be explored, Elmore explains, "Mapmakers would include a drawing like this to communicate the message: Over here—this land is a known world. But up there—we don't know what exists. It's unknown territory. Be afraid. Be very afraid."[3] Elmore uses this analogy to explain the state of schools today, where leaders need to "recognize what changes you must make to lead and equip a new generation of emerging adults who live in the corner of the map."[4] This is especially true if we as educators have gotten used to receiving turn-by-turn directions from the tried-and-true voices in our field, whose advice worked well for times that were more stable or predictable. But now, as Elmore explains, "making new maps is an art we must learn."[5]

Fortunately, we learned something about this art in a previous two-year collaborative project that resulted in the book *MindShift: Catalyzing Change in Christian Education*.[6] With the help of Rex Miller, a futurist and pioneer of the MindShift process of sector-level transformation, we learned the importance of finding outliers—those few who have already taken steps off the map, or have marched off entirely—and understanding their stories. In the process of writing the book you now hold, we visited eleven Christian schools and networks that have transformed their structural, financial, or operational models with the goals of long-term sustainability and increased missional reach. More than tweaking a practice or process here or there, these schools and networks have engaged in fundamental mindset changes about what it means for Christian schools to be future-ready.

The stakes are high when it comes to transformational decisions like the ones that the schools in our study have made. And yet as Beerens and Ellefsen point out in regard to change in Christian education, "It is a risk to try new things, to move in new directions . . . but we have reached a time in history where by not innovating we are running a greater risk than staying our current course."[7] We hope the stories and strategies in this book will inspire leaders of Christian schools to think innovatively, strategically, and above all, missionally about long-term sustainability. Reaching future generations with the love of God through healthy, thriving Christian schools is well worth the risk.

—Lynn Swaner, Jon Eckert, Erik Ellefsen, and Matthew Lee
Fall 2022

INTRODUCTION

Educators spend much of their time ensuring that their students are prepared for the world they enter after graduation. Leaders at private schools must also ask whether their schools themselves are future-ready—meaning are they positioned financially, structurally, and programmatically for the long-term? The question of future readiness for Christian schools is at the forefront of many leaders' minds: at the close of the 2019 Global Christian School Leadership Summit, over eleven hundred Christian education leaders named sustainability as the "number one priority that Christian schools need to tackle right away."[1]

Research shows their concern is warranted, as challenges to Christian school sustainability in the United States have been well-documented in recent years. For example, research conducted by Barna Group and the Association of Christian Schools International (ACSI)[2] points to two macro trends that are impacting Christian education: the changing faith profile of parents, in which the number of self-identified Christians is shrinking, particularly among millennials;[3] and the proliferation of school options, such as public charter schools and online academies.[4]

In 2019, ACSI launched a multi-year initiative to address the challenge of Christian school sustainability.[5] The initiative received generous grant funding from a private family foundation and the Christian Education Charitable Trust of the Maclellan Family Foundations. In partnership with Cardus, ACSI designed a two-year research project in which a team of ACSI research staff and Cardus senior fellows visited schools across the United States to understand innovative approaches to sustainability challenges. The findings of this project help to answer the question of how Christian schools can leverage innovative missions and models for future readiness.

Framing the Sustainability Challenge

The sustainability challenge for Christian schools is multifaceted and results from both external and internal factors influencing the sector. These challenges can be categorized into the following broad headings: enrollment, reach, innovation, and human resources.

Enrollment

Over the last five decades, the number of families that enroll their children in private elementary schools has been in significant decline among middle-income families, with the gap in enrollment rates between high- and middle-income families widening from 5.5 percentage points in 1968 to 9.3 in 2013. Should these trends continue, it is possible we may see similar declines in independent middle and high schools as well.

Private schools often point to need-based financial aid as the key to accessibility for more families. However, data from ACSI shows that, at the fiftieth percentile, the amount of need-based assistance per recipient in ACSI schools is less than a third of the tuition cost.[6] Further, the relationship between school size and aid has historically been *inverse*—meaning that the larger the school, the lower the percentage of students receiving need-based tuition assistance (23 percent of students at schools enrolling 100 students or fewer receive this aid, which drops to 12 percent of students at schools enrolling 701 students or more). These data points could suggest that financial accessibility challenges to Christian school enrollment are not adequately overcome by financial aid.

One possible mitigating factor is the unprecedented increase in school choice monies becoming available across the United States.[7] This trend is encouraging, with the promise that more families from diverse socioeconomic backgrounds will have access to private schooling. However, Christian schools will need to be both ready and willing to receive these funds—let alone compete among many viable educational options that these funds will make accessible to students and families—as well as appropriately support the students and families who take advantage of them.

One-third of Christian schools saw an enrollment bump from fall 2019 to fall 2020, much of which may be attributed to families switching from public to private schools during the COVID-19 pandemic.[8] While encouraging, the data suggest that the gain was most often modest, in the 5–10 percent range; moreover, at the same time, over half of Christian schools saw an enrollment decline during that period, which resulted in an average of 3.2 percent decline in enrollment across the sector. This reality, combined with the historical decline in private school enrollment and continued financial pressures for middle-class families, makes it unlikely that enrollment gains due to the pandemic will be either permanent or widespread across the sector.

Reach

While Christian schools face an enrollment challenge as a sector, they also face a reach challenge. Historically speaking, the Christian school sector has underserved several types of students, families, and communities. These underserved groups represent not only possible untapped market reach for Christian schools but also "misses" in terms of the great commission to make disciples (Matthew 28:19–20), and the greatest commandment to love one's neighbor as oneself (Mark 12:31).

The first group of underserved students and families are those who either are not professing Christians and/or do not attend a local Protestant church. Sixty-four percent of Christian schools require at least one parent to be a professing Christian and regular church attender, and an additional 17 percent require the same of both parents. Just 19 percent of Christian schools accept students from families with any or no religious affiliation.[9] These admission requirements are typically in line with the school's philosophy and historical identity, either as a "covenant" school that partners with Christian families in the education and discipleship of their children, or a "missional" school that seeks to reach its community with Christ-centered education.[*] It should be noted that the line between these philosophies and their admission-related policies is increasingly blurred. For example, many schools waive faith-related admissions requirements for international students, and some schools use a "blended" approach, with target percentages for students who come from Christian families and those who do not.

The second group of underserved students, families, and communities are those from racial or ethnic minorities. While student demographics are considerably less diverse in private schools as compared with public schools,[10] the numbers are starker at Christian schools,[11] as shown in figure 1.

The reasons for this are likely many. Some reasons may be related to geography and related demographics—for example, most Christian schools are located in suburban or rural areas, which may themselves not reflect the broader diversity of the overall population. Another contributing factor, as already discussed, may be the funding models of private schooling in the United States, which limit access for families of lower socioeconomic status; given the well-documented economic inequality between people of color—particularly African Americans and Latinos—and whites,[12] this may amplify access issues

---

*Schools may use other terms (such as "discipleship" or "community-based") to denote their philosophy and related admissions practices.

Figure 1. Student Race/Ethnicity by School Type

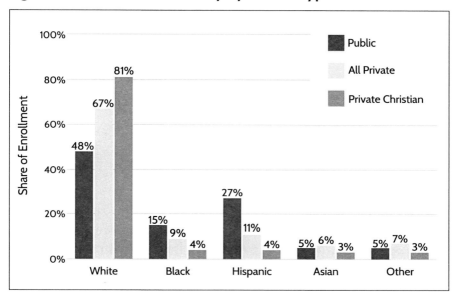

Note: Categories used here are defined according to the National Center for Education Statistics (NCES).
Sources: Public and private school data from NCES, "Racial/Ethnic Enrollment in Public Schools," The Condition of Education in 2020: Elementary and Secondary Enrollment, 2020, https://nces.ed.gov/programs/coe/pdf/coe_cge.pdf; private school data from NCES, "Private School Enrollment," The Condition of Education: Private School Enrollment, 2021, https://nces.ed.gov/programs/coe/indicator/cgc; Christian school data reported by ACSI, "2018–2019 Tuition & Salary Survey Member Report," Association of Christian Schools International, 2019, at the fiftieth percentile.

for those racial and ethnic groups. Finally, there may be institutional reasons that can deter students of color from applying, enrolling, and remaining at Christian schools,[13] such as a lack of teachers of color,[14] a lack of culturally appropriate curricula and materials, and differences between students of color and their white peers' perceptions related to racism and discrimination.[15] Whatever the confluence of these and other factors, the reality is that the Christian school sector is not fully reaching students and families of color.

A third group of underserved students are those with special needs. Only a third of Christian schools offer a special education program or related services, and the median percentage of the student population participating in those programs is seven[16]—exactly half that of public schools, where the average percentage of the student population who received special education services during the 2019–20 school year is fourteen.[17] Moreover, 40 percent of these Christian schools indicate they have enrolled students with known special education needs beyond what their schools currently are covering.[18] Low numbers of Christian schools offer other programs serving students with other needs, such as gifted, talented, or honors students (33 percent); students with physical disabilities (6 percent); and students pursuing trade/vocational training (4 percent). While each of these programs requires an investment of financial and staffing resources, a number of Christian schools are finding that not only is such an investment possible but also that it enables schools to enroll all siblings (versus just some) from current school families—thereby increasing enrollment with mission-appropriate students whose families are already committed to the school.[19] And during the COVID-19 pandemic, schools that reopened on campus with increased support for special education were among those who saw enrollment growth, averaging close to 10 percent.[20]

Innovation

In addition to both enrollment and reach challenges, the Christian school sector is also facing challenges related to educational transformation, including rapid technological innovation and diversification of learners and their needs. Research suggests that Christian schools have historically been slow to identify and implement innovative and research-based practices.[21] It is perhaps unsurprising, then, that in the field of innovation and school improvement, "virtually no contributions have been made in that knowledge domain with respect to the effectiveness of Christian schools."[22] This is problematic not only because research has demonstrated that innovative practices in education are correlated with educational effectiveness[23] but also because innovation is necessary to adapt to the changing educational environment in which all schools find themselves today.[24]

Regarding practices at Christian schools, only around a third offer innovative programs like those for non-traditional students (e.g., homeschool or part-time students) or online course or program offerings.[25] In early 2020, the COVID-19 pandemic spurred widespread shifts in educational delivery, with over 80 percent of Christian schools pivoting to online learning within five days of physically closing in spring 2020.[26] However, it is questionable how truly innovative schools' approaches were, as the top two delivery methods for online learning were the use of Zoom or other videoconferencing tools (71 percent of schools, across all grade levels) and teacher-recorded videos (also at 71 percent); after a notably significant drop-off, the third most-employed tool was Google Classroom (at just over 56 percent).

Furthermore, follow-up survey data reveal that most schools (just over 55 percent) plan to discontinue their distance learning options past the pandemic, with an additional 30 percent planning to keep current options in place, and under 15 percent planning to expand them in some way.[27] Possible reasons for this retrenching in educational delivery may include insufficient staffing or expertise, a steep learning curve to transition from emergency distance learning to a high-quality offering, prohibitive cost in terms of technology investment, or concern about undermining the traditional brick-and-mortar financial model. Regardless, the question of what to do with existing distance learning options is just one of many facing schools in a post-pandemic world—but Christian schools must be willing to seize the opportunity to spur further innovation. As a report from the Christensen Institute observed, "There is an opportunity—and arguably an imperative—for schools to pursue lasting, positive change during this period of instability. It's tempting to see crises as an inevitable harbinger of change. But innovations implemented in response to today's crises aren't guaranteed to last into tomorrow."[28]

Human Resources

Even before the COVID-19 pandemic, research on the Christian school sector documented widespread stress among both teachers and leaders,[29] as well as high turnover in school leadership and compensation rates that are significantly below that of other educational sectors.[30] When taken together, these factors suggest that Christian schools are facing a human resource challenge that may undermine their long-term sustainability.

Research on the impact of COVID-19 suggests that this challenge has reached acute levels during the pandemic, with the top two concerns reported by Christian schools being overwork of teachers and staff (77 percent of schools) and the mental health of leaders, faculty, and staff (73 percent). Despite this concern, only 13 percent of schools have an intentional plan in place to support faculty and staff in the area of well-being, while two-thirds (66 percent) indicated they are "doing some things" to support faculty but have not developed an intentional plan, and around one-fifth (21 percent) reported that they are "not really doing much" to support faculty in these areas.[31]

These findings are certainly not unique to Christian schools. Across the field of education, teacher burnout, attrition, and shortages loom large.[32] And difficulty retaining school leaders has been exacerbated further by the challenges of leadership during a politically and culturally contentious time.[33] While schools cannot change external factors like pandemics or politics, their cultures, environments, structures, and practices are within their control. Established and reinforced over time, these internal factors serve as assets or detriments to the well-being of teachers and leaders and are key to addressing the human resource challenges facing Christian schools.[34]

From Challenges to Opportunities

These challenges to Christian school sustainability—enrollment, reach, innovation, and human resources—are complex and systemic. The models and structures that have historically characterized Christian schooling appear increasingly inadequate to handle these challenges. If sustainability is defined as maintaining the way Christian schools currently operate, these challenges appear insurmountable. However, a powerful means of moving forward involves redefining sustainability as ensuring that the school's *mission* continues into the future, instead of preserving the way schools look and function today. Viewing sustainability from this missional (versus institutional) perspective can prove generative not only for finding innovative solutions to these challenges but also for transforming them into opportunities for mission-driven growth.

As already mentioned, research suggests that Christian schools have historically been slow to identify and implement innovative and research-based practices.[35] However, several innovative, counter-normative models of school finance and structure—and the schools pioneering them—have recently been identified as part of a two-year transformational MindShift in Christian Education project.[36] These innovative approaches include technology-enabled delivery systems, mergers and acquisitions, cost and resource sharing, entrepreneurship and third-source income, boutique programs, school choice funding, wrap-around programs, school networks and districts, and innovative community partnerships.

Exploring these and other innovative models holds significant value for Christian schools that are seeking approaches to long-term sustainability. However, rather than a technical "how-to" understanding, a vista on how schools have transitioned to these models—and away from more traditional ones—is needed for at least two reasons. First, simply replicating approaches from one school to another is largely ineffective in school change.[37] And second, innovation goes beyond simply implementing a specific practice to developing a cultural orientation toward change; as the authors of *Collective Genius: The Art and Practice of Leading Innovation* explain, "Instead of trying to come up with a vision and make innovation happen themselves, a leader of innovation creates a place—a context, an environment—where people are willing and able to do the hard work that innovative problem solving requires."[38]

The Study

With generous grant funding and in partnership with Cardus, ACSI conducted a two-year research project to identify and examine innovative financial and structural models that contribute to Christian school sustainability while expanding educational access for underserved students, families, and communities. The purpose of this research was fivefold:

1. Identify innovative Christian school financial and structural models that contribute to long-term school sustainability while expanding educational access for underserved students, families, and communities;

2. Determine key change processes, practices, and conditions that school constituencies cited as important in moving from traditional to innovative models;

3. Identify key barriers or challenges that schools encountered in implementing innovative models;

4. Describe how school constituencies understand the shift to innovative models as related to the mission of their Christian schools; and

5. Examine the leadership dispositions and behaviors that contribute to success in implementing innovative models.

The current study builds on work from the United Kingdom[39] and Canada[40] conducted in the Christian school sector. These studies used a similar case study methodology with an appreciative inquiry (AI) frame.[41] According to Stavros, Godwin, and Cooperrider,

> At its heart, AI is about the search for the best in people, their organizations, and the strengths-filled, opportunity-rich world around them. AI . . . is a fundamental shift in

the overall perspective taken throughout the entire change process to "see" the wholeness of the human system and to "inquire" into that system's strengths, possibilities, and successes. . . . AI is being used worldwide in both small- and large-scale change initiatives across every type of organizational sector.[42]

Selecting the Schools

During the spring and summer of 2020, the research team identified and secured consent from ten schools, plus one network of schools, to participate in the study. These eleven sites were identified through the MindShift in Christian Education research and network. All sites were selected for participation using purposive sampling, based on the following criteria:

1. Schools or networks of schools are located in the United States and serve a range of grades anywhere between kindergarten and twelfth grade (for example, K–8, 9–12, K–12).

2. Innovative models used by schools or school networks must fall into one or more of the following categories: mergers, voucher programs or school choice networks, property ownership and leasing, online or hybrid programs, micro-business hubs, or closely related categories.

3. The innovative model of school finance and structure must be in operation at the time of study and must have served as one of the school's or school network's primary business or operational models for no less than two years at the time of study—meaning that the model is not in a pilot phase or limited in scope compared to the rest of the school's or network's operation.

4. The innovative model must have as one of its goals the inclusion of students, families, and/or communities typically underserved by Christian private schools (as defined by recent research) and/or by the specific school or network of schools being considered for participation in the study.

Additionally, all schools were examined using Independent School Management's "sustainability markers," identified as correlated with "private schools' ability to sustain excellence in student programs."[43] These include consistent donor cultivation, development office capacity, meaningfully competitive faculty salaries, perceived adequacy of employee benefits, enrollment demand in excess of supply, internal marketing, master property or facilities plan, quality of facilities, and strategic plan/strategic financial plan. While two of the markers—related to cash reserves and the percentage of school's operating expense that is covered by billable monies or funds transferred from interest-bearing accounts—were not used as exclusion criteria, participating schools or networks were screened for financial health, including a track record of balanced budgets and steady growth.*

Conducting the Research

During the 2020–2021 academic year, the research team conducted document analyses of school climate surveys, student data, program planning documents, committee work products, student achievement data, and school improvement plans. The team held Zoom interviews and focus groups with school leaders, board members, administrators, faculty, staff, and community members affiliated with the schools or school networks. A quantitative survey was also administered to leaders, faculty, and staff at all participating schools (see appendix for survey methodology and findings), the results of which helped to inform the semi-structured protocols for responsive interviewing.[44]

With the easing of COVID-19 travel restrictions, visits to all eleven sites occurred during fall 2021. During the visits, the research

---

*This is because excluding schools or networks of schools based on these two markers would automatically eliminate some that would have non-traditional financial models. For example, schools that prioritize underserved students often have fewer cash reserves and a more limited traditional donor base; however, these schools are often approaching revenue generation in innovative ways that better serve longer-term sustainability, within their contexts, through increased access.

team conducted in-person interviews, focus groups, and classroom observations to facilitate triangulation.[45] Data analysis and report writing were conducted during early spring 2022, with participants at each school invited to review drafts of the research reports and provide feedback for accuracy and resonance.

Three Themes

The study focuses on the change processes that schools employ as they move from more traditional models of school finance and operations to more innovative approaches. The findings of this project are organized into three themes:

1. The first theme of *Mission and Culture* reveals the ways that schools in the study prioritize distinctiveness, relevancy, and inclusion as means of ensuring their missions continue.

2. The second theme, *Structures and Practices*, encompasses how schools resource creatively, reimagine structures, and take disciplined risks, as they have implemented non-traditional models of school finance and operations.

3. The final theme, *People and Community*, points to the ways that schools prioritize their staff, invite partnerships with the community, and share innovation with other schools in their ongoing efforts toward sustainability.

Taken together, these themes illustrate how Christian schools have not only addressed the challenges to Christian school sustainability—including enrollment, reach, innovation, and human resources—but also transformed them into catalysts for mission-driven growth and readiness for the future.

About the Schools

Chattanooga Christian School (CCS) was founded in 1970 and is located in Chattanooga, Tennessee. CCS is a Christian interdenominational, coeducational, K–12 day school that serves over fourteen hundred students on a main campus with three emerging microschools in other neighborhoods of Chattanooga. The school has been an innovator through a community watershed project, their redevelopment of a car dealership for their facilities, a specialized learning center and inclusion services, and the development of local microschools in partnership with area churches.

Christian School Association of Greater Harrisburg (CSAGH) was founded in 2017, when Harrisburg Christian School (founded in 1955) acquired West Shore Christian Academy (1973) to create a unified Christian school district in the Capitol District of Harrisburg, Pennsylvania. The two schools remain distinct entities in different communities that are located on opposite sides of the Susquehanna River. The acquisition allowed CSAGH to grow to 770 students from seven counties and demonstrates the possibility of a district approach to Christian schooling that may generate greater efficiencies, productive collaboration, and overall better Christian school health within a given geographic region.

Cincinnati Hills Christian Academy (CHCA) was founded in 1989 with multiple campuses in suburban Cincinnati, Ohio. CHCA is a Christian non-denominational, college-preparatory school ranging from PK2 to twelfth grade, educating over thirteen hundred students. CHCA consistently supports new innovations as they have a teacher innovation fund and developed an entrepreneurship and sustainability program. CHCA expanded their reach to downtown Cincinnati through their Armleder campus, which is located in the historic Crosley Square Building.

The City School is a PK–12 multi-site Christian school in Philadelphia, Pennsylvania, that resulted from the merger of three schools. Beginning in 2006, Spruce Hill Christian School (founded in 1978) joined with City Center Academy (1983). Eventually, the two schools came to be unified under The City School name in 2013, and in 2014 Philadelphia Mennonite High School (1998) joined the new merger.

The City School currently educates over four hundred students on the Spruce Hill Campus (K–5), the old Philadelphia Mennonite High School campus now known as the Fairmount Campus (PK–5), and the newly purchased Poplar Campus (6–12). Throughout the merger process, The City School developed innovative approaches to creating efficiency, but most significantly The City School became a reflection of Philadelphia, with its educational and core commitments reflecting its mission of flourishing students, schools, and neighborhoods throughout the city.

Grand Rapids Christian Schools is a multisite school system in Grand Rapids, Michigan, that came from the merging of a number of Christian schools over the past century. Grand Rapids Christian Schools serves twenty-three hundred students across five campuses in neighborhoods throughout the city: the elementary school's Iroquois Campus (grades PK–4) and Evergreen Campus (PK–5); Rockford Christian School (PK–8); Grand Rapids Christian Middle School (5–8); and Grand Rapids Christian High School (9–12). In the early 2000s, Grand Rapids Christian Schools was in a state of crisis with significant debt and declining enrollment, particularly in their elementary schools located in neighborhoods located throughout the city. Since that time, Grand Rapids Christian Schools has regained a position of financial strength by becoming an innovator in creating new financial systems, merging schools to develop a multi-dimensional system, making a commitment to greater inclusion of students of all abilities, and being an incubator for curricular and school change.

Hope Academy was founded in 2000 and is a K–12 Christian classical school in the Phillips neighborhood of Minneapolis, Minnesota. Hope educates 550 students by fundraising a significant portion of tuition through a student sponsorship model. Not only is the school using an innovative funding approach, but they also lease a portion of its facility to other social services organizations and has developed the Spreading Hope Network to found other urban Christian classical schools throughout the United States.

HOPE Christian Schools (HOPE) is a part of a larger organization known as Open Sky Education. The first HOPE Christian school was founded in Milwaukee in 2002 as a grade 1–4 school that accepted vouchers from the Milwaukee Parental Choice Program. Today, HOPE operates six K–8 schools in the Milwaukee area serving approximately thirty-five hundred students, with expansion plans for at least three more campuses in the near future. In addition to HOPE schools, Open Sky Education operates charter schools in Arizona and the St. Louis area, offers a wraparound character education program, and is working to develop a microschool-based delivery model for Christian education.

Lynden Christian Schools (LCS) was founded in 1910 by a community of Dutch Reformed immigrants and is a PS–12 Christian school near the US-Canada border in Washington state, just south of Vancouver, British Columbia. LCS educates over twelve hundred students and has consistently been an innovator in this rural community. Because they are a "parent-run" school through an elected board, LCS focuses on partnerships with families to educate all students in a cost-effective manner, which has driven their innovations in career and technical education, agriculture education, inclusion and learning services, a Spanish immersion program, and creative financial support structures through a thrift store and multiple financial assistance programs.

Oaks Christian School was founded in 2000 as a co-educational, college-preparatory, Christian school in Westlake Village, California, just north of Los Angeles. Oaks Christian annually enrolls nearly fifteen hundred students in their on-campus day and boarding school. Although Oaks Christian currently offers grades 5–12, in spring 2022 the board of trustees approved expansion plans to add grades PK-4. Since its inception Oaks Christian has been known for their college-preparatory and athletic success; however, as they continue to grow they've sought innovations to extend the impact of their school with the development of an online school, opening of dorms for domestic and international residential students, creation of the IDEA (Innovation,

Design, Engineering and Aeronautics) Lab, and the development of individual learning pathways through the opening of three Institutes (Global Leadership, Arts and Innovation, and Engineering). Another aspect of Oaks Christian's innovative approach is the repurposing of old business facilities that were primarily used in the production of missile-defense systems in the 1980s.

Valley Christian Schools (VCS) was founded in 1975 as Youngstown Christian School. In 2015, the school was renamed to reflect their changing nature as multi-site with locations throughout the tri-county area of Youngstown, Ohio. Currently, the school educates more than seven hundred students across the Lewis Center for Gifted and Learning (a 3–8 school in downtown Youngstown), the Pleasant Grove Campus (a K–2 school), and Central Campus (the primary 3–12 school). Valley Christian Schools has innovated new ways to achieve their mission through the opportunities presented by the Ohio EdChoice Scholarship program.

Valor Christian High School opened its doors in 2007 in Highlands Ranch, Colorado, a growing suburb south of Denver. Valor was founded to be a Christian school unlike any that existed in Colorado and to become a model for future Christian schools throughout the United States. Valor currently educates twelve hundred students and is known for its athletic success but also for being an educational innovator. Valor's dynamic educational environment has spawned the Valor Conservatory for the Arts with professional sound, dance, recording, and production studios; the Valor Institute for Applied STEM, which reflects the growth of STEM businesses in Denver; Valor Discovery, a service and intercultural learning program; and the Valor Sports Network, which produces Valor athletic events.

PART ONE
MISSION AND CULTURE

CHAPTER ONE

BE DISTINCTIVE

What do you *want*? That's the question. It is the first, last, and most fundamental question of Christian discipleship. In the Gospel of John, it is the first question Jesus poses to those who would follow him. . . . This is the most incisive, piercing question Jesus can ask of us precisely because we *are* what we want. . . . You are what you *love*.

—James K.A. Smith, *You Are What You Love*[1]

Our wants, our desires, and our loves shape everything we do. They shape our daily lives, as well as our long-term plans. They shape our priorities and our choices. They shape the bounds of what we are willing (and unwilling) to do. Over time, what we love shapes our identity—who we are, and what we're known for.

Organizationally, what do we love? That may seem like a strange question to ask; we don't normally think of schools as loving something. Yet in reality, most schools articulate their deepest desires through their mission and vision statements. Of course, the degree to which schools live out, and into, their mission will vary from school to school. But for schools that are "Mission True"—a term Peter Greer and Chris Horst coined in *Mission Drift*—the organization's mission is the North Star.[2] A school's mission, what it loves and seeks at the deepest level, is what makes the school distinctive. All schools have teachers and students, all have curricula and learning goals, and most schools (though not all) have buildings and campuses. The school's mission should differentiate that school from others, with those differences manifested in all that it prioritizes, creates, resources, and evaluates.

Asking what we love organizationally may also seem like an odd place to start a discussion of school sustainability. And yet, our research revealed that this question is exactly the place to start. In fact, most of the findings in this study hinge on how schools answer this question. We found that when schools love the mission that has been entrusted to them, they are willing to go to great lengths—often in very innovative ways—to achieve it. As Greer and Horst explain, "Being Mission True isn't synonymous with being unchanging. On the contrary, remaining Mission True will demand you change to continue to fulfill your mission."[3]

We found that when schools love the mission that has been entrusted to them, they are willing to go to great lengths—often in very innovative ways—to achieve it.

We found this to be true for all of the changes that schools were willing to make in this study—whether merging with another school from a different Christian tradition, forming partnerships with community agencies, starting an inclusion program from scratch, or moving from a predominantly tuition-funded school to almost entirely voucher funded overnight. Love for their mission is what propelled these schools to act boldly even when it wasn't easy, conventional, or necessarily safe. As the epilogue to *MindShift: Catalyzing Change in Christian Education* makes clear, "Deep love compels deep action. To love is to risk."[4]

While all of the schools in this study embodied missional distinctiveness, this section highlights five schools' stories that demonstrate how this distinctiveness correlates with a willingness to innovate programmatically, structurally, and financially. The experiences of these schools—which are diverse geographically, in price point, and in the students they serve—suggest three elements that are key to this innovation: (1) gaining missional clarity, (2) refusing to compromise the mission, and (3) taking the long view. And in turn, as schools have leaned in to each of these, they have experienced demonstrable increases in missional sustainability.

Missional Clarity: Sustainability's Ground Floor

Logically speaking, in order to sustain something into the future, we must first know what it is. While this seems self-evident, many schools lack clarity around their mission and what makes them distinctive from other schools. In our study we found that gaining missional clarity contributed directly to two schools' sustainability, both in terms of righting the ship financially and creating new opportunities for growth and expansion.

Oaks Christian School (Westlake Village, California)

Oaks Christian School was founded in 2000 as a co-educational, college-preparatory Christian school in Westlake Village, just north of Los Angeles. Oaks Christian annually enrolls nearly fifteen hundred students in its on-campus day and boarding school. Although Oaks Christian currently offers grades 5–12, in spring 2022 the board of trustees approved expansion plans to add grades PK–4. Oaks Christian's mission statement is "to dedicate ourselves to Christ in the pursuit of academic excellence, artistic expression, and athletic distinction, while growing in knowledge and wisdom through God's abundant grace."

Despite the high level of specificity evident in the school's current mission statement, the school's story suggests this wasn't always the case. A few years back, during a time of significant leadership turnover, the school experienced a lack of clarity around the mission. When Rob Black was named the new head of school in 2015 after serving as the school's CFO and then interim head, there was a period of reasserting the Christian mission and values of Oaks Christian. At the time, it became clear that the school needed to double down on its mission, or "stand firm to stand out." With the board's reaffirmation of the school's Christian beliefs and values, an advisory board was created as a feedback loop, which allowed leadership to confirm and reinforce the essential direction of the school. While some school stakeholders feared the potential for enrollment loss and decreases in donor interest, both have actually increased since clarifying the distinctives of the school, with strong support from the broader Christian community.

Through a collaborative and iterative process, the school leadership and board identified what the school describes as Oaks Christian's "three pillars": "academic excellence, artistic expression, and athletic distinction, built upon a biblical worldview and Christ-centered foundation." One administrator confirmed that "we have a clear mission, which is known by our faculty, our staff. It's not just collecting dust on the wall. We know it, we can recite it." The mission guides hiring as well as students' experiences, as leaders and teachers work with students to "find out where their passion is" and plug them into the right program. Per the administrator, the school's clarification of their mission led to the creation of "these [individual learning] pathways where you can go try things and figure out your passion, whether it's arts, academics, athletics—any one of our pillars, or a combination of them."

Further, missional clarity has enabled a willingness to change. As Black explained, "It is said all the time on our campus that we can pivot so long as we remain true to the school's mission." Pivoting has led to the development of new opportunities to fulfill the mission, which are concurrently providing new sources of income. One example is the development of three academic "institutes" (in global leadership, arts and innovation, and engineering) where students pursue individualized learning, engagement with professionals and experts in the field, and real-world experiences. As an administrator explained, these institutes allow students to "dive deep" into their elective studies.

Beyond academic programs, Oaks Christian's missional clarity led to the creation of an entirely new structural innovation: in 2011, the school launched Oaks Christian Online, with middle and high school programs that use both live and asynchronous instruction. An administrator explained that this online school is geared toward "students looking for more flexibility over when, where, and how they learn," including missionary families, international students, and students or parents who are professional artists or athletes, with the goal of "being able to deliver a blended product that allowed students to go chase their dreams, whether it's in acting or in sports or something else, or following their parents around the globe."

Although the online diploma costs significantly less than the traditional brick-and-mortar version, the school reports that initial fears of the online program "cannibalizing" the on-campus student body proved to be unfounded. Rather, the program created an additional financial "lever," by increasing access for families that would have never considered Oaks Christian previously, including those who have geographic, financial, or lifestyle reasons to consider an online program. Other Christian schools across the country also now partner with Oaks Christian to offer their online program to their own students but under their own school brand. Thus, the missional clarity gained at Oaks Christian resulted in not only deepening the school's offerings but also expanding their reach beyond their community—all of which contributed to greater financial sustainability.

The City School (Philadelphia, Pennsylvania)

Located on the opposite coast, in the city of Philadelphia, The City School is a PK–12 multi-site Christian school that came from the merger of three schools. In 2006, Spruce Hill Christian School (founded in 1978) joined with City Center Academy (founded in 1983), and in 2014 Philadelphia Mennonite High School (founded in 1998) joined the new merger. The City School currently educates over four hundred students from socioeconomically diverse backgrounds, with the mission "to train students' minds, disciple their hearts and bring light to the city—one child at a time."

When school parent Jake Becker became the head of school in 2010, the merger of Spruce Hill Christian School and City Center Academy was four years old. Becker shared that while the school had a "great academic and cultural environment," there were some issues left to resolve from the merger; specifically, there was a need to align the school's "mission, money, and message." According to Becker, not only were both campuses unclear on the identity of the whole school, but also there were "two stories" told at the school: the first was a story of urban blight, often used in fundraising efforts; and the second, communicated to prospective parents, was the school's mission of excellence. Early in his tenure, Becker met with key board members who were part of the merger, to clarify the school's mission: "I asked them, 'I need to understand who are we, as an organization?' And they had never been asked that question." Becker tied this lack of missional clarity to a commensurate lack of clarity around decision-making and organizational structure. Together, Becker and the board decided that "if we didn't know the answer, we needed to figure it out."

The process of gaining missional clarity was intensive, as Becker explained: "We hammered on words so hard, talking about what we cared about the most. That passion is what would drive people. We had to be really specific and articulate it well." Ultimately, the school determined its mission was to provide both educational *excellence* and *access* to children in Philadelphia, in Jesus's name. With this clarification, Becker explained, he was able to lead forward with the support of the board, as it "facilitated one big question after another." Missional clarity led to decisions like raising tuition by 30 percent, which was staged over multiple years and was used to improve programs and buildings as well as broaden the socioeconomic diversity by offering more financial aid.* It also led to changing the name of the school to The City School, to reflect both the unified nature of the campuses as well as the school's mission to serve the diverse communities of Philadelphia.

In 2014, bolstered by this missional clarity, the school began considering an additional merger in order to realize the possibility of having a centralized upper school campus with neighborhood-based elementary campuses. Becker explained that leading up to the merger, "I talked with people for a long time about our core commitments, and how those core commitments could apply to any Christian school in the country." Although The City School's theological background was Reformed, the school board entered into discussions with Philadelphia Mennonite High School regarding merging. The Reverend Leonard Dow, who currently serves as a board member and also was on the board during the merger, described how the two schools came together over what unified them: "I suggested to them that Scripture could be used as a common denominator, not as a divisive tool." From the Presbyterian side, the theological emphasis on the ministry

The school leadership continues to see missional clarity as key to the future, not just as an important part of the school's history.

of reconciliation matched well with the Mennonite emphasis on shalom—providing common theological ground. When the two schools ultimately merged, shalom was officially added as a core commitment for the school. As Dow explained, "Shalom is obviously a big part of

---

*Importantly, this tuition increase did not affect students accessing state or local funds to attend.

what the school is about, and plays into the environment of the city in which we're in. . . . That became a rallying cry for us that we're engaging young people on the academic side, on the spiritual side, so that they can be the light of Christ directly—the *shalom* in the city of Philadelphia."

The school has seen continued growth in enrollment as well as donors since the merger. The school leadership continues to see missional clarity as key to the future, not just as an important part of the school's history. Joel Gaines, who succeeded Jake Becker as The City School's leader, explained that in recent years "we have buckled down. There's an intentionality to really home in on the things that we've been doing well and go deeper—not just wider, not just brighter or shiny. This idea of our core commitments . . . going deeper with the things that we say we believe." Standing out in Philadelphia—with Jesus, excellence, access, and *shalom* as its distinctives—The City School has provided a unifying vision for donors and families to join in while seeking to contribute to the flourishing of neighborhoods throughout the city.

Don't Compromise the Mission

As Greer and Horst explain in *Mission Drift*, "Everything flows from *why*. Not only does it motivate others to join you, it also guides what you do—and often more important—what you *don't* do."[5] One school in our study started in 2000 with crystal-clear clarity on their mission—but notably, this didn't just include what they would do, but also what they would *not* do. This determination to not compromise on their mission led to the school's creation of a unique and remarkably different financial model.

Hope Academy (Minneapolis, Minnesota)

Just over twenty years ago, Hope Academy was founded as a K–2 Christian classical school in the Phillips neighborhood of Minneapolis. Currently, Hope educates 550 students in grades K–12 from the inner city in keeping with its mission "to foster hope in God within the inner-city neighborhoods of Minneapolis by providing youth with a remarkable, God-centered education." While Hope educates traditionally underserved students, Russ Gregg, school co-founder and head of school, was adamant that students receive a high-quality, college-preparatory education. Their mission includes three main thrusts: holding high expectations for urban youth, holding staff accountable to those expectations, and providing support to reach those expectations.

But the school's mission is as much about what the school will *not* do. Gregg frequently and adamantly says, "We do not give kids a hot dog education." He explained the reference as the typical food served by church groups when they minister in urban settings, because "hot dogs are both inexpensive and convenient, and easy to do." When the co-founders were looking to start an urban school in Minneapolis, Gregg said, "The question was, what kind of education should we serve to our neighbors? The significant temptation was well, a 'hot dog' education. But the call was to serve your neighbors, to love them, as you love yourself. And so then the question was, well, did we want a hot dog education for our [own] kids? And of course, not a single one of us does."

Thus, the mission of the school was clearly articulated back in 2000—to provide a college-preparatory education to urban youth, without compromising on quality. But given "the enormous cost to give to my neighbors the same kind of education that I wanted for my own children," the financial challenge to meeting this mission was formidable, according to Gregg. To solve this challenge, he explained, "What we did was we look at the typical model of a private school where the parents pay 90 percent or more of the tuition costs, and we gave it what we call the 'kingdom flip.'" This flip involved scholarship partners who pay 90 percent of a student's tuition, with a current total of approximately four hundred partners who each contribute $7,500 each year. This innovative financial model also had a kingdom purpose, as Gregg explained, referencing Luke 14:15–24: "It's really a carrying out of what Jesus told us when he told a parable about giving a banquet. He said, when you give a banquet, don't invite just your friends and neighbors and relatives who can pay you back. He says, instead, invite the poor. Then you'll have real treasure. And that's been our experience—that is what Hope Academy is spreading every day, a rich educational banquet for those that would otherwise never, in their wildest dreams, believe that they have a seat at the table."

From a sustainability perspective, this financial model prevents the school's reliance on a handful of big donors, government funding, or other sources, which if withdrawn could jeopardize the school's financial model and students' education. Key to the success of this model is the importance the school places on relationships their partners have with the students that they are sponsoring. As one school administrator explained, "We invest a lot of effort at connecting that person who's giving the scholarship with the student who's benefiting from it. And when you see how you are personally changing the life of a neighbor right through this gift, you're not going to walk away from that lightly." As Gregg described it, "That was the insight that opened the door of this kind of education to everybody."

Even twenty years after its founding, refusing to compromise on the mission remains critical for Hope Academy. Gregg explained that for long-term sustainability that is aligned with the school's mission, "keeping laser-focused on the mission, and bulldogging the mission, is a key thing." Gregg shared that to this end, the school is "guarding against mission drift" through very specific admissions parameters. This includes a policy that 75 percent of the student body must meet the financial and at-risk profile that undergirds the partnership model. Gregg described the reason behind this policy: "Sometimes your own success becomes one of your biggest threats. We could probably enroll quite a few more families who would not meet those poverty or risk profiles. But that would significantly shift the focus of our work. This policy, to hold oneself to that kind of a governor, has been very, very helpful because we could change the whole makeup of the school quite easily." In keeping with this policy, when students apply who do not fit the profile of the school (generally meaning that their families can afford to pay more than 10 percent of the tuition), Hope Academy leaders will refer them to other high-quality educational options in the city.

While these parameters help ensure that they keep their mission in focus and that they do not compromise for the sake of growth, Hope Academy is far from constricted in its reach. This missional clarity, coupled with their innovative funding approach, gave Hope Academy both the vision and margin to develop the Spreading Hope Network to start other urban Christian classical schools. Founded in 2016, the network supports leaders around the United States with training and consultation around starting a new urban school, as well as support during the launch year. The network uses much the same financial model as Hope Academy, with financial partners coming alongside leaders to provide support as they plan and launch new schools. For Hope Academy and the schools planted through the Spreading Hope Network, refusal to compromise the mission has contributed to both long-term sustainability and growth.

Take the Long View

Finally, the story of two schools in our sample suggests that missional distinctiveness requires taking the long view , in two unique contexts: first, when changing demographics appeared to threaten a school's historical model of over thirty years; and second, when a newly founded school put guardrails in place to preserve and protect the school's distinct mission into the future.

Valley Christian Schools (Youngstown, Ohio)

Valley Christian Schools (VCS) was founded as Youngstown Christian School by the Highway Tabernacle Assembly of God in 1975 (see photo insert). The founding pastor of the church was interviewed in a local newspaper article at the time and shared a vision for students of all racial, ethnic, and socioeconomic backgrounds coming together to learn at a Christian school in the city. Although this was the founding vision for the school, the following three decades saw enrollment from predominantly middle-class, white students from Christian families. The financial model of the school—tuition-driven with scholarships for families from the sponsoring church—both matched and reinforced such demographics.

This enrollment pattern changed in the early 2000s following a capital campaign to build a new high school. The new high school building opened in 2006 with only eighty-six students—not nearly enough to sustain the school or service debt. School leaders visited local churches to promote enrollment, but there was a lack of interest on the part of suburban families. Michael Pecchia, the current president of the school, compared this to Jesus's story of the banquet in Luke 14 (just like Russ Gregg from Hope Academy): although they had been invited to enroll at the new high school, the "traditional" families the school had historically served did not come.

At the same time the high school opened, Ohio's Educational Choice Scholarship Program (commonly called "EdChoice"*)—which at the time provided students from designated public schools the opportunity to attend chartered non-public schools—was introduced. The new scholarship program provided a way for families who were previously unable to access Christian private schools to attend VCS. The leadership believed that God provided a way for the "underserved and uninvited" to attend. Shelley Murray, head of schools, described the process the board and leadership used to make the decision as "asking—why are we doing this? Ask what the mission is intentionally. If you don't ask it, the person with the loudest voice will lead." By asking this question and clarifying their mission in the process, the board and leadership decided to take the latter option of enrolling

---

*Ohio's EdChoice scholarship program is distinct from the Indianapolis-based research and advocacy organization of the same name.

scholarship-eligible families of low socioeconomic status from Youngstown. As a result, the school began to serve a new demographic of students. With families paying 20 percent of tuition, and the remaining 80 percent paid through the scholarship—the school essentially flipped its traditional financial model, where families paid 80 percent of tuition and aid covered the remaining 20 percent.

This transition was not without its challenges, as the leadership reported that it raised big "who are we?" questions for staff, with significant teacher turnover ensuing. But the school continued to lean into the new model and saw significant growth and impact over the next decade. In 2013, the Educational Choice Scholarship Program expanded to include all students from low socioeconomic backgrounds and not just students from designated public schools, which opened the door for even more students to attend. In 2015, the school was renamed from Youngstown Christian School to Valley Christian Schools, to reflect the changing nature of the school and the multiple communities it serves throughout the tri-county area of Youngstown. Currently, the school educates more than seven hundred students at three campuses, with a 92 percent retention rate across all grades.

Along with its new name, in 2015 the school adopted the mission, "Love More. Expect More. Be More." The school's website explains that this mission "relates to nurturing the spirit, challenging the mind, and serving the world; three simple values that have guided the dramatic change process" the school underwent. At the same time, it could be said that the school itself now loves more students, expects more of itself as a school, and *is* more—in terms of significance and impact on its community. Over forty years after its founding, the school better reflects the founding pastor's vision as a diverse school that serves students of all backgrounds. It also enrolls far more students, with greater financial stability, than at times in its past. As such, the school serves as an inspiration to schools in urban settings across the country facing similar demographic shifts—not to view these shifts as threats to their institutional history, but to seize them as opportunities to fulfill their mission with even more students in need of a Christian education.

Valor Christian High School (Highlands Ranch, Colorado)

Valor Christian High School opened its doors in Highlands Ranch, a growing suburb south of Denver, Colorado, in 2007. The goal of the school's founding families was that Valor would be unlike any Christian school that existed in the state and would become a model for innovative Christian schools throughout the United States. As articulated by the founders, Valor's vision is to "prepare tomorrow's leaders to transform the world for Christ," and its mission is to "in partnership with committed parents . . . provide a purpose-driven college preparatory program, within a vibrant Christ-centered environment that empowers students to discover their passions and to develop their unique gifts and abilities while growing in wisdom, knowledge, leadership, faith and service."

According to the founding head of school, Kurt Unruh, "Pursuing our mission and vision has been a clarion call from our founders." Unruh explained that "blue ocean thinking"—that is, innovation and entrepreneurism—"was really our foundation—at the very core of who we were." Valor's dynamic educational environment has spawned a host of innovational programs for its twelve hundred students, including the Valor Conservatory for the Arts with professional sound, dance, recording, and production studios; the Valor Institute for Applied STEM, which reflects and engages with the growth of STEM businesses in Denver; Valor Discovery, a service and intercultural learning program; and the Valor Sports Network, which produces Valor athletic events.

According to Unruh, "Because Valor is not that old, we have our founders primarily still involved and in place, reminding us constantly what that initial vision and mission of the school was." But in 2017, ten years after the school opened, this founding group was keenly aware that they would eventually need to give governance control to a future generation of leaders and community members, but at the same time desired to have accountability to the founding story, vision, and mission of the school. Thus, as the founding board determined that they would gradually make a transition into an oversight role, a new board chair was named who was not a founder and additional board members were added. At the same time, the board changed their by-laws to create a distinct class of "voting members" composed of four of the founding families. These voting members were not members of the board, but were given the charge and power to approve or disapprove of several key attributes of governance, including the appointment of board members, approving any new head-of-school appointment, changes to governance documents, taking on debt, and other major financial decisions. In essence, these founders placed upon themselves the responsibility for long-term commitment to mission and vision, while ceding daily oversight and control of board functions.

As the youngest school in our study, Valor is still early in its institutional journey. At the same time, Valor's founders demonstrated a future-mindedness in desiring to guard the school's mission and its distinctives. This early part of Valor's story may be useful for newer schools or for those leaders who are looking to found new schools. Along with missional clarity and refusal to compromise the school's distinctives, installing missional guardrails early in a school's life may turn out to be a generative practice for long-term sustainability.

Know What We Love

Greer and Horst explain that Mission True organizations "distinguish between guarding the mission and guarding the means."[6] A key question for schools looking toward sustainability is, Do we love the mission that God has entrusted to us—or do we love the means we are using to achieve it more? This is not a rhetorical question, but rather one for deep reflection. As James K.A. Smith warns, "You might not love what you think."[7]

For the schools in our study, loving their mission more than the means led them to make radical changes, like transforming an educational delivery model to include an online school; implementing a radically non-traditional financial model; crossing theological and historical divides to merge schools and better serve an entire city; and completely changing the student population that had historically been served by the school. Gaining missional clarity, refusing to compromise the mission, and taking the long view all contributed to the demonstrable increases this group of schools experienced in enrollment, donor contributions, community impact, and national reach.

Even these laudable gains are not ends in and of themselves, however. As Jake Becker, former head of school, shared, "The City School is not permanent. No school is permanent, just like no society is permanent. The City School is God's tool to serve kids for as long as God wants to do that." Ultimately, increased sustainability represents an expansion of schools' ability to fulfill their God-given missions—along with the opportunity for even greater faithfulness in loving God, his mission, and all those they are called to serve.

CHAPTER TWO

BE RELEVANT

Our mission, in light of the current environment we find ourselves ministering within, is to present a Christianity that is as concerned with human flourishing as it is with doctrinal orthodoxy. . . . The gospel should meet people at the point of their deepest confusion and at the height of their loftiest ideals.

—Christopher Brooks, *Urban Apologetics*[1]

God's Word is both eternal (Isaiah 40:8) and eternally relevant (Hebrews 4:12–13). The Christian schools in this study are relevant to their communities because they are standing firm on the timeless truths of the gospel. At the same time, like the good Samaritan in Jesus's parable (Luke 10:25–37), they do not cross to the other side of the road when they see their neighbors in need. Instead, precisely *because* of the gospel's relevance to their community, Christian schools seek to love and serve their neighbors by meeting them where they are at. True relevancy for Christian schools means being both firmly grounded in their Christian mission, as discussed in the preceding chapter, *and* being dynamic and responsive to the opportunities God presents for them to serve the common good.

For the schools in this study, being relevant in this way led to shifts in programming, resources, and messaging to better serve the needs of their communities through Christian education. In addition to increased opportunities to be the salt and light of Christ to their neighbors, the resulting kaleidoscope of educational options they created in the process has drawn even more families to the school. Using this definition of relevancy, we identified three elements among the schools in this study: (1) *knowing* the community they serve by being aware of needs related to demographics and urbanicity, (2) *growing* with their community by adapting with changing community profiles, and (3) *listening* to their neighbors by relentlessly seeking and acting on community feedback.

Know the Community

Being relevant within a community involves knowing the needs of that community. This is particularly true of three schools in our study—one in a rural context, and two in large urban centers.

Lynden Christian Schools (Lynden, Washington)

We begin on the West Coast in rural Lynden, Washington, which is primarily a ranching and farming community that is buffered from the urban growth of the Vancouver-Surrey metroplex because of the US-Canada border. Lynden Christian Schools (LCS) has been serving its community for close to one hundred years and was originally founded by Dutch Reformed farmers who settled in the area. As the school has grown over the decades and expanded the student population it reaches, it continues to respond to the needs of the surrounding community it serves. Recently, this has included reimagining and redesigning its Career and Technical Education (CTE) program. In response to Washington state emphasizing a need for the development of increased CTE training to meet the job needs of the state, the school convened a CTE committee to meet with local farmers and business owners to focus their program. As a result, they have reimagined what might have been a more traditional vocational-technical program into an innovative and developmental hands-on CTE program, which includes classroom learning combined with innovative projects and on-the-job experience. For example, LCS students are an integral part of the on-campus greenhouse and plant sale that they host on campus.

Through this effort, the school has facilitated opportunities for their students to be creators, developers, and leaders within the vocational careers their community needs as the students are provided skill development in small engines, welding, and construction while problem-solving with local companies. Likewise, the school has a historically strong agriculture program and they have expanded opportunities for middle school students. By expanding the agriculture and CTE programs, LCS is innovating course offerings to align student interests in agriculture and veterinary science through the National FFA Organization (formerly Future Farmers of America). The domino effect of partnering with the community to provide professional opportunities leads to curricular and programmatic changes that required facilities adjustments, including renovating an old woodworking shop to create a multi-dimensional CTE space and redesigning and expanding the school's greenhouse. Thus, the school's efforts to be responsive and relevant have resulted in a reshaping of its programmatic offerings and its physical campus, all while continuing to stand firm on a century of Christ-centered education that serves its unique community.

The City School (Philadelphia, Pennsylvania) and Oaks Christian School (Westlake Village, California)

The City School in Philadelphia and Oaks Christian School outside of Los Angeles, both introduced in the preceding chapter, are schools in urban centers that have cultivated reciprocal relationships with their communities, in an effort to both serve their neighbors and connect their students with the rich resources of their cities.

The City School is a three-campus school in three unique sections of the city with each neighborhood providing cultural richness and a wide range of learning opportunities. The opportunities are not without their challenges as many students take public transportation and then have to walk several blocks to get to the combined middle and high school campus. Serving students in an urban center requires particular attention to the needs of the community, but school leaders see these needs as an opportunity to seek the *shalom* of the city. In fact, The City School sees itself as part of the fabric of the neighborhoods and city it serves. That service is tangible in the form of renting its gym for use by a neighborhood basketball program, hosting three local churches on their campuses for Sunday services, and housing a neighborhood daycare facility in one of the upper school's wings. The school has also partnered with Marc Vetri, a celebrity chef and award-winning restaurateur based in Philadelphia, to offer cooking classes to its middle schoolers and to serve as a site for Vetri's educational filming projects.

In addition to these everyday opportunities to be a good neighbor to their community, The City School has also opened its doors when its neighbors have faced challenges and tragedies. For example, when a charter school up the block from the Poplar campus lost heat in the middle of the winter, the principal knew he could walk down the street and ask for The City School's help; Joel Gaines, head of The City School, invited the charter school students and staff in to use their cafeteria for classes and a pick-up space for the day. And when a devastating fire in the Fairmount neighborhood took the lives of twelve people, including eight children, the nearby Fairmount campus of The City School offered up the school basement to receive overflow donations for the families. This level of service to one's community requires deliberate effort as well as a posture of openness to the opportunities that God provides. Through it all, The City School has become increasingly known in the city of Philadelphia as a school that is not only an integral part of the community but also a good neighbor to all with whom they share a block or a neighborhood.

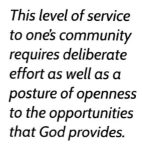

This level of service to one's community requires deliberate effort as well as a posture of openness to the opportunities that God provides.

On the opposite coast, due to their proximity to Los Angeles, Oaks Christian School can tap into high-level experts to serve as advisors for their three academic institutes (arts and innovation, global leadership, and engineering), thereby ensuring that the skills, knowledge, and habits of mind their students are developing are not only relevant but also on the cutting edge of industries. For example, a University of Southern California professor and advisory board member co-designed a business class for Oaks Christian, and through partnerships with Spotify and Skype, Oaks Christian teachers and students are collaborating with students and advisors in Sweden through songwriting and digital production. Because of the diverse influences on the direction of programs, the school is finding that they have individual students who are talented in disparate areas like improvisation and engineering, and who flourish in their intersection.

This in turn is reshaping their campus facilities; Oaks Christian purchased a pet food facility that became their ten-thousand-square-foot innovation space, called the IDEA (Innovation, Design, Engineering and Aeronautics) Lab, which is now a state-of-the-art fabrication and production facility. Teachers and several students have gone through weeks of professional training programs to use the lab's complex tools, with students now building an electric car, designing robotics, and creating with 3D printing (see photo insert). A day before the site visit for this study, the chief innovation officer of NASA Jet Propulsion Laboratories had visited the IDEA Lab and had determined that it was the only non-university partner they would pursue because of the quality of the facilities, faculty, and students. These and other partnerships between industry leaders and students are sparking innovation that enhances relevance for students' learning and relevance for what the school can contribute to the community.

Grow with the Community

While the mission of a given Christian school stands firm throughout the years, the community served by that school can often change drastically from one decade to the next. For three schools in this study, a key part of being relevant has been growing with their communities.

Chattanooga Christian School (Chattanooga, Tennessee)

Chattanooga Christian School (CCS) is located in Chattanooga, Tennessee, a mid-sized city that is growing both in population and in diversity. The school serves the multi-dimensional needs of its community as it changes rapidly and significantly. As the community has changed, the school itself has expanded its community partnerships to develop programs in the areas of inclusion and disability, health and wellness, and neighborhood education needs. One example of this is The Learning Center, which is a partnership with the Siskin Children's Institute for students in grades 6 to age twenty-two who have significant learning and developmental needs. Through this partnership, CCS can tap into the expertise of the Institute's therapy services while using their own expertise in educational and social programs to expand their mission of partnering with families to provide a Christian education for more students. The Learning Center can serve up to thirty-two students who the school would not have been able to serve on its own. Serving students with diverse learning needs has become part of the school's identity; as one school leader shared, "This is not optional. It is part of who we are." This is evident in their demographic numbers, with 20 percent of the school's students being served by a 504 plan or individualized education plan.

CCS also desires to become more racially and ethnically diverse to better reflect the city of Chattanooga. To this end, they have developed purposeful marketing and outreach along with strategic scholarship programs that are supported by $2.4 million in financial assistance. However, as the school reached capacity, school leaders identified that particular communities were unable to afford CCS's tuition or they did not have access to the school's location. Therefore, over the past five years, school leaders met with over one hundred community leaders to develop neighborhood microschools to provide a CCS education in partnership with local churches. By partnering with churches in different neighborhoods of the city, a CCS education is becoming increasingly relevant for larger sections of the city at a fraction of the cost of the tuition on the primary campus.

There are now three microschools in operation, but the first that launched is The King School located at Olivet Baptist Church in downtown Chattanooga. Olivet is a historic black church with a rich history in the civil rights movement. While the church provides the space, CCS provided support in helping to fundraise the resources needed to upgrade the church facilities to house a school. In addition to hiring, training, and paying the salaries of all teachers and staff, the school also provides all of the microschools' marketing and back-office support. Although the price point is significantly lower than the tuition at the CCS main campus, the curriculum and resources are the same. According to The King School's principal, the microschools "give students a full education. We don't give them second-hand things." In the fall of 2021, the school had just opened its second microschool in a converted K-Mart. The new school, Purpose Point Learning Academy, provides early childhood education in partnership with Mount Canaan Church, which shares the space. The church and community saw early childhood education as a need in the most economically depressed neighborhood in Chattanooga, and with this partnership, CCS has stepped into that gap—being responsive to the needs of its growing community and reaching more children with a quality Christian education.

Cincinnati Hills Christian Academy (Cincinnati, Ohio)

Cincinnati Hills Christian Academy (CHCA) was founded in 1989 and operates multiple campuses in northern Cincinnati, among them the downtown Armleder campus, which opened in 2000 in the historic Crosley Square Building. CHCA is a Christian non-denominational, college preparatory school ranging from PK2 to twelfth grade, educating over thirteen hundred students. While the school has a heritage of seeking and incentivizing innovations, their Entrepreneurship and Sustainability Program is a tremendous example of how a Christian school can grow alongside its community with a willingness to develop new programs, facilities, and community connections to better serve its students and neighborhood.

The program started close to ten years ago with humble beginnings when a teacher and a group of students launched a coffee cart business called The Leaning Eagle, named after the school's mascot. The coffee cart began with gross sales of $15,000 by delivering coffee to students and faculty before and after school and at school events. During this start-up season, the team faced many challenges, including nearly being shut down due to a lack of awareness of health code requirements. But over time, the coffee cart grew into what is now the Leaning Eagle Coffee Bar; located at the entrance of the school, the student-run business is ethically sourced coffee and grosses $50,000 per year (see photo insert).

Students and faculty did not stop there, however. What began as a coffee cart has grown into a business incubator that seeds resources for other entrepreneurial ventures. The school has a dedicated director of entrepreneurship and sustainability at CHCA, Stephen Carter, who has spearheaded the building of a teaching kitchen that is attached to its on-campus Eagle Farms and Greenhouse, where they are growing organic fruits and vegetables using aeroponic, hydroponic, and soil-based growing systems. Students both sell their produce to the community and use it in their teaching kitchen, which is run by a graduate of the school who is an executive chef. Through the teaching kitchen, they are exploring cuisine from around the world and sharing their products with the community. For example, on Fridays, using produce from the greenhouse, students make wood-fired pizzas that they sell to students and the community. Through related classes, they are integrating science, business, entrepreneurship, and marketing.

The student-run businesses that the school incubates are held to high standards for both business integrity and environmental stewardship. The school's website points out that the Entrepreneurship and Sustainability Program is "more than just a business class." Instead, it is a robust initiative that combines innovation, real-life learning, leadership development, business and management skills, and environmental sustainability goals in an effort to not only train student leaders but also connect with and serve its community.

Grand Rapids Christian Schools (Grand Rapids, Michigan)

Grand Rapids Christian Schools provides a compelling lesson in growing with a changing community. The institution has been in operation for more than 130 years and is the combination of a number of Christian private schools that ultimately came together in stages. The school now educates twenty-three hundred students across five sites throughout the city: the elementary school's Iroquois Campus (grades PK–4); the elementary school's Evergreen Campus (PK–5); Rockford Christian School (PK–8); the middle school (5–8); and the high school (9–12). A unique feature of the school as a multi-campus school is the distinctive nature of each school and how each campus has a level of autonomy to innovate. For example, the Evergreen Campus classrooms are multi-aged, the pedagogy is built around "inquiry learning" using a modified school calendar, and it will apply for the International Baccalaureate Candidacy (Primary Years Program) in 2022. To meet another community need, the Evergreen

Campus is also in the process of opening an Early Learning Center for children between eighteen and thirty-six months of age, which will be open for current and other non-attending neighborhood families. The Iroquois Campus offers a Spanish Immersion program that begins in preschool and now continues through high school graduation for interested students, and Rockford Christian School offers outdoor and environmental education as a significant part of preschool to eighth-grade students' educational experience.

Similarly, the high school is connecting students to the local community via their Winterim program, through which students can take courses, participate in service trips, or do internships. Specifically, a broader multidisciplinary project titled Gone Boarding—which is a combination of design arts, industrial arts, physical education, and business—grew from a Winterim class. As originally designed, the course was focused on snowboarding, but grew into the regular curriculum where students can design, build, use, and sell a variety of boards including snowboards, skateboards, and longboards.

The school's ability to grow with its community is evident not only in its programs but also in its physical buildings. The newest, the Iroquois Campus, was built on the site of a former public high school in a historic neighborhood that had served the community since 1925. The fact that many of the residents of the neighborhood attended that high school gave a high degree of local attachment to the site. Recognizing its importance, school leaders and architects engaged the community in the design process to ensure the building reflected the community's values while keeping architectural components such as pillars and stonework from the original school. A two-story stained-glass window depicting the connections between the former school with the community embodies the school leadership's attention to historical and communal detail (see photo insert). Likewise, internal artifacts were used from the multiple Christian schools that were merged over decades to form Grand Rapids Christian Schools, so that alumni of those schools could easily see their experiences as now part of the larger school story. The new Iroquois Campus was a significant investment that reflected the value of connecting past, present, and future, as well as understanding Grand Rapids, the particular neighborhood, and the relevance of the school's mission to the community.

Listen to the Community

Both knowing and growing with one's community are both predicated on the final element that emerged from the school stories shared in this section: *listening* to the community. This involves schools' regularly seeking and acting on community feedback, with a willingness to change and evolve based on the needs their communities identify. Some of the feedback school leaders receive comes from walks around the neighborhood, while other feedback is collected systematically and quantified. In our survey, we found that having a close connection with the community was a robust predictor of a respondent's optimism that the school would be open and more accessible in ten years.

Some of the feedback school leaders receive comes from walks around the neighborhood, while other feedback is collected systematically and quantified.

For example, Cincinnati Hills Christian Academy's evolving entrepreneurship program is built entirely on feedback and student interest. Multiple iterations of businesses and ideas have come and gone over the last decade. One year, students decided to start a smoothie business that struggled; at the end of the year, the business was scrapped as students realized that the location of the business, tight margins, and limited appeal made the business unprofitable. This type of "failing forward" was a powerful lesson in entrepreneurship for the students and represents the way the school seeks and acts on feedback in tangible ways. Similarly, Lynden Christian Schools has recently shuttered a long-standing recycling program that was historically highly valued by the school community. When the program lost its financial viability due to decreased market demand for recycled materials, school leadership decided to repurpose the recycling center, possibly to expand into sales of construction materials or to provide a multi-use space for the school's growing CTE programs.

At Oaks Christian School in California, two new initiatives demonstrate their responsiveness to community needs. As a result of feedback from students and families, Oaks Christian has developed a student learning center that provides additional support for classes and college admissions exams that is housed in a separate building on campus. The center is available to all students, but Oaks Christian also makes it available to local families who are interested in paying for the additional support. This broadens Oaks Christian's reach to include more community members. Oaks Christian also recently renovated and repurposed dorm space to house over 150 domestic and international students from seventeen countries; the redesign was based on student feedback and is now complete with a kitchen, study spaces, dining areas, movie viewing areas, and game rooms to make students feel comfortable in a collegiate-type space. Launching this during a pandemic has been challenging, but the two new facilities offer opportunities for increasing Oaks Christian's relevance and sustainability within their local community and well beyond.

Along with these findings from the study's qualitative interviews and focus groups, the results of the quantitative survey pointed to the importance of feedback to ensuring schools' relevance to their communities (see the appendix for survey methodology and overview of findings). First, administrators who responded to the survey agreed most strongly with the statement "Our school regularly solicits feedback for improvement from the school community." Second, administrators who welcome feedback also seemed more likely to support relevant innovation. And third, respondents who report that they "welcome change" are also significantly more likely to state they expect their school to be open ten years from now as well as more likely to be accessible to more students.

While remaining true to their mission, the schools in our study are adapting to meet the aspirations of the communities they serve by offering different programs, opportunities, and learning experiences for students. Ultimately, the most important feedback comes from students who are thriving in new offerings that allow them to develop their God-given gifts in ways that are relevant to them and their communities.

CHAPTER THREE

BE INCLUSIVE

The countercultural message that the church preached in the ancient world was that all people are fundamentally equal due to their being bearers of the divine image. It was the ancient message and should also be the modern message of the church today.

—Irwyn L. Ince Jr., *The Beautiful Community*[1]

In the very first chapter of the Bible, we learn that God created humanity in his image. This theological concept of *imago Dei*, or the divine imprint on the life of every human being, can be viewed as the basis for many of the Bible's commands—such as loving one's neighbor as oneself (Mark 12:31), avoiding partiality (1 Timothy 5:21), and advocating for those who "cannot speak for themselves" (Proverbs 31:8–9). And ultimately, it culminates in the presence of individuals from all "tribes and peoples and languages" in heaven (Revelation 7:9). Until then, however, our societies, churches, and even our schools grapple with disparities and divides of all kinds in their communities.

In the introduction to this study, we highlighted the specific challenges faced by the Christian school sector in reaching students from lower socioeconomic backgrounds, students of color, and students with disabilities. In this chapter, we briefly discuss the efforts of the schools in this study relative to the first two groups of students and then focus most extensively on the latter. This is for a few reasons. First, we explore financial models for increasing access for students from diverse socioeconomic backgrounds at length in other sections. Second, while the schools in this study did not have comprehensive initiatives to increase access for students of color, a number have developed some intentional efforts with dedicated staff, which we note. And finally, the inclusion of students with disabilities is where some schools in the study have gone to great lengths to change structures, partner creatively, and innovate their programs; thus, there potentially may be much to learn from these inclusion efforts in terms of what it would take to welcome and intentionally support underserved students, both with and without disabilities.

Socioeconomic Inclusion

Most Christian schools offer some type of financial aid to those families who cannot afford to pay the full price of tuition. However, as mentioned earlier, data from ACSI shows that, at the fiftieth percentile, the amount of need-based assistance per recipient in ACSI schools is less than a third of the tuition cost.[2] Further, the relationship between school size and aid has historically been *inverse*—meaning that the larger the school, the lower the percentage of students receiving need-based tuition assistance (i.e., 23 percent of students at schools enrolling 100 students or fewer receive this aid, which drops to 12 percent of students at schools enrolling 701 students or more).

These data points suggest that accessibility challenges to Christian school enrollment are not adequately overcome by the traditional model of financial aid. Rather than accepting this complacently, several schools in this study developed significant approaches to socioeconomic inclusion: first, innovations to financial and structural models, which increase financial accessibility; and second, the use of school choice programs and monies. For example, as described previously, Chattanooga Christian School has offered strategic scholarship programs that are supported by $2.4 million in financial assistance and widely marketed to their community. However, with the school reaching capacity and tuition still out of reach for many families, school leaders developed a microschool strategy in partnership with local churches. With the price point of tuition significantly lower than that of CCS's main campus, the microschool partnership enables Christian schools to operate in some of the most economically disadvantaged neighborhoods in Chattanooga, thereby reaching more children through Christian education. In Minneapolis, Hope Academy's innovative partnership model—where around four hundred partners each contribute $7,500, or 90 percent, of annual tuition for a student—enables students who need significant assistance to access a quality Christian education in the urban context.

Accessibility challenges to Christian school enrollment are not adequately overcome by the traditional model of financial aid.

In addition to these models, a number of schools in our study have taken advantage of school choice programs, which have increased dramatically in the United States—from five programs in 2000 to twelve in 2010, and up to twenty-nine in 2021.[3] This growth suggests that school choice monies may be available to more families who would choose to send their children to Christian schools if those schools are ready and willing to receive them. One school and one network of schools in our study have school choice monies as their primary funding source. First, as already shared, in 2006 Valley Christian Schools began enrolling families with 80 percent of their tuition paid through the then-new Ohio EdChoice scholarship program. In 2013, the program expanded to include all low-income students and not just students from designated public schools. And second, Open Sky Education operates a network of seven K–8 HOPE Christian Schools in Wisconsin serving approximately thirty-five hundred children, as well as public, open-admission charter schools in Arizona. As Andrew Neumann, Open Sky's executive chair and CEO, explained, "Making a full, lasting education—including the three pillars of academics, character, and faith—as accessible and affordable for all: that's the mission."

Racial and Ethnic Inclusion

A second group of underserved students, families, and communities at Christian schools are those from racial or ethnic minorities. As discussed in the introduction to this study, while student demographics are considerably less diverse in private schools as compared with public schools,[4] the numbers are starker at Christian schools.[5] This is undoubtedly related to the funding models of private schooling in the US, which limit access for families from lower income brackets; given the well-documented economic inequality between people of color and whites,[6] this may amplify access issues for those racial and ethnic groups. There are also likely institutional reasons that can deter students of color from applying, enrolling, and remaining at Christian schools,[7] such as a lack of teachers of color,[8] a lack of culturally appropriate curricula and materials, and differences between students of color and their white peers' perceptions related to racism and discrimination.[9]

While the reality is that the Christian school sector is not fully reaching students and families of color, most Christian school educators would agree that having a student body and faculty that is representative of its surrounding community, including in terms of race and ethnicity, is desirable. Moreover, there is compelling research that suggests that racial and ethnic inclusion in Christian schools is beneficial for all students. For example, ACSI's Flourishing Schools Research found an inverse relationship between flourishing outcomes for students and the degree of insularity of a school's culture (with insular culture defined as a lack of diversity in the student body, lack of engagement with the surrounding community, and shielding of students from the outside world). Conversely, alumni of Christian schools where leaders intentionally engage the community are 50 percent more likely to report they're currently walking with God.[10]

Several schools in this study had designated staff or committees who were tasked with community-building efforts, which included shaping the school environment and culture to be supportive of students. This included roles like a director of community (Hope Academy in Minneapolis), a director of student experience (Valor Christian High School in Colorado), a director of diversity and belonging (Cincinnati Hills Christian Academy in Ohio), and a board-appointed cultural competency committee supported by a three-year contract with an outside consultant (Grand Rapids Christian Schools in Michigan). Some schools, like The City School in Philadelphia, engaged staff in diversity and cultural sensitivity training. Interestingly, these five schools differ in their urbanicity (three suburban and two urban) and student body composition (three with a predominantly white student body, and two predominantly enrolling students of color). This suggests that the question of belonging is not unique to a specific type of Christian school but rather may be an area of dedicated and increased focus for schools across the sector.

Inclusion of Students with Disabilities

Historically, the main barriers to the inclusion of students with disabilities in Christian schools have been limited financial resources to implement adequate support systems, a lack of a clear framework for inclusion, and limited access to information about effective inclusion models.[11] Some recent data suggest that these barriers are closer to being crossed, however. First, with public spending on special education students in relative decline,[12] families are increasingly looking to private schools, including faith-based schools, for solutions. And with the prevalence of private school choice programs increasing nationwide, "parents want control of the special education dollars to obtain the best services possible whether in public schools, private schools or behavioral clinics."[13] Moreover, research suggests that private schools—such as those in Florida that access the John M. McKay Scholarships for Students with Disabilities Program—can spend significantly less per pupil (close to $10,000) on special education services than public schools, and yet deliver higher levels of parental satisfaction.[14]

There is a growing awareness and use of clear frameworks and models for inclusion in Christian education.

In addition to these compelling financial reasons for inclusion—increasing parental demand and cost-effectiveness of private schools educating students with disabilities—there is a growing awareness and use of clear frameworks and models for inclusion in Christian education. In this study, we found multiple schools partnering with the All Belong Center for Inclusive Education (formerly the Christian Learning Center Network), whose mission is to equip schools "to glorify God through purposeful, innovative inclusion of persons with varied abilities" and which offers consultation, an accreditation standard, and a wide range of resources to assist schools in their journey toward inclusion. In this chapter, we highlight the well-established special education and inclusion practices of two of these schools, Grand Rapids Christian Schools and Chattanooga Christian School, with particular attention to how their program innovations have helped make their schools more accessible and sustainable.

Grand Rapids Christian Schools (Grand Rapids, Michigan)

For Grand Rapids Christian Schools, the motivating factor to pursue inclusion was fulfilling their mission and their commitment to the families with whom they had already formed partnerships. While it may have created opportunities to expand enrollment, the vision for their schools to be inclusive communities drove their innovations in special education. Kim Primus, PS–12 director of inclusion services, said of students with disabilities, "We're not whole if they're not here. Inclusion changes the culture in the school. It is a blessing for all." As Primus reflected on the beginnings of special education at Grand Rapids Christian Schools, "We wanted families to be able to educate all of their children together."

Grand Rapids Christian Schools currently has close to six hundred students receiving some level of learning support through their Educational Support Services, which includes support by aides in a combined push-in and pull-out format. An additional fifty students receive inclusion services; these students have a range of disabilities including cerebral palsy, Down syndrome, developmental delays, echolalia, emotional impairment, hearing impairment, non-verbal sensory processing disorder, spina bifida, and visual impairment. Despite this current range of disabilities the school accommodates, it did not build its highly regarded special education programs overnight. As Primus said, recalling being approached to serve as an inclusion aide for a student with a visual impairment, "I thought, 'I don't know anything about visual impairment. I don't know how to Braille.'" But she saw past the challenges and remembered the mindset of finding a way to support all students: "I took two years of online Braille classes so that I could work with the student and support her well." Primus went on to serve as an inclusion aide, then as an inclusion coordinator, and finally as the director of inclusion. Throughout this journey, Primus explained, "I've always felt empowered by [our superintendent] and our campus principals." The leadership team's shared vision for inclusion has been key to culture change at the school; to this day, school leaders include Primus in the hiring process as well as strategic plan development.

A successful special education program needs a champion like Primus as well as leaders to provide support from the top, but it also needs a team to carry out the mission. Over time, the school started hiring its own inclusion coordinators and special educators, who work collaboratively with teachers to meet students' needs. Relationships form the central tenet for the school's five pillars for inclusion and, reflecting the school's shared value that all children are fearfully and wonderfully made, educational plans are student-centered and take into account students' strengths and needs. Staff members work intentionally with families, seeing parents as partners in the process for identifying supports that a student requires. For students, Eagle Circles and Eagles Links are peer groups that are formed to foster community, belonging, and genuine friendships. On the instructional side, the culture of inclusion is vertically aligned, from campus to campus, with the director of inclusion services meeting regularly with each inclusion coordinator to ensure there is a common mindset on each campus. And they support their teachers in their work with students by providing professional development.

On the financial side, tuition equity—or not charging additional fees for inclusion services—is an important part of serving whole families and building an inclusive culture in which students and their families feel as though they belong. "Families with exceptional children have a lot of financial pressures, emotional pressures, future pressures that other families don't have," said Primus. "It's a way to partner with families and to say we truly love and care, not only about your child, but also about you as a family." Leadership again played a critical role for Grand Rapids Christian Schools to adopt a policy of tuition equity. "We had a well-attended board meeting at which a number of families were saying it isn't right," Primus recalled. "We shouldn't have families who have children with disabilities paying additional fees to attend school. And so from 1996 to present day, our students all pay the same tuition."

Grand Rapids Christian Schools also accesses publicly supported resources that can help Christian schools as well, and to that end partners with some local public schools for services. Depending on a student's disability and the given state's Tax Equity and Fiscal Responsibility Act or Katie Beckett Waiver, therapy and other medical services may be covered by the state and federal Medicaid program. Far from just resources for inclusion, these opportunities to partner with local districts and agencies offer a chance for the school to stand out in its inclusion mission; as Primus said, "These specialists tell us we've got something special going on because of the way we advocate for our students."

"Special education is necessary, not optional . . . It blesses our entire school community, not just the students it directly affects."

Finally, at Grand Rapids Christian Schools, building a budget follows the vision that special education is integral to the mission of Christian education. Support for each student is determined by asking what the student needs, not what the school can provide. The budget for inclusion is calculated "not at the student level, but at the school level," explained chief financial officer Jim Primus. "It's because we believe that special education is necessary, not optional, and that it blesses our entire school community, not just the students it directly affects."

Chattanooga Christian School (Chattanooga, Tennessee)

Like at Grand Rapids Christian Schools, the pursuit of inclusion at CCS was centered on fulfilling its mission and partnering more fully with existing families. "To turn away students who are part of a Christian family who have siblings who attend here simply because of their ability feels wrong and contradictory," stated Shonda Caines, CCS's director of exceptional education programs and lower school head. "Our special education program and services help us serve whole families. That's what our families look like. That's what our churches look like. And we feel that that's what our schools should look like." For Caines, this mission was not only professional but also personal: as the parent of a student with Down syndrome and autism, the school's special education programming allows Caines's youngest son to attend the same school as his three older siblings.

In the middle of CCS's campus stands The Learning Center, an over-thirty-nine-hundred-square-foot, state-of-the-art learning facility that first enrolled students for the 2021–2022 school year. According to the school's website, "The Learning Center provides a truly individualized, comprehensive, educational program for students grades 6 and up who have more significant needs." It meets these students' needs through a partnership with the Siskin Children's Institute, which offers consultation and integrated therapy services, and CCS, which provides educational and social programs. Strictly speaking, The Learning Center is not an example of inclusion. But it has helped the school become more accessible and more sustainable. "It helps us serve a different population than we've been able to serve before," said Caines.

One of the remarkable things about The Learning Center is how CCS has been able to offer the program while maintaining a policy of tuition equity. The Center boasts a low student-teacher ratio, individualized attention to student needs, and therapeutic services through the Siskin Children's Institute, all of which incur additional costs. But for most families, the costs for these services, above and beyond the general education tuition, can be covered through Tennessee's Individualized Education Account (IEA) program. Tennessee is one of fifteen states that offer a private school choice program designed to benefit special education students, and its IEA program is available for families once enrolled in the public school system who felt that the school did not meet the educational needs of their exceptional child. This program enables families to take their child's Basic Education Program dollars to a local private school that better serves their needs. This program's allocations vary from district to district, but average roughly $7,000 per year—approximately the cost of additional services through The Learning Center.

Thus from a budgeting standpoint, building special education programs has enabled CCS School to access revenue sources that were previously unavailable. Notably, The Learning Center "has allowed CCS to reach out to donors and grant-funding organizations that wouldn't have been interested in us otherwise, but want to support this type of program," Caines shared. The Learning Center was launched in part with the support of a generous donor who made clear that they were not from a Christian background and didn't intend to donate to the school again in the future, but shared in the vision for establishing an innovative special education center in Chattanooga. In addition to private donors, the Christopher and Dana Reeve Foundation offers Quality of Life grants that are specifically designed to "empower individuals with disabilities and their families." The Maclellan Family Foundations, located in the heart of Chattanooga, partners with CCS as well.

Building an inclusive culture takes intentionality and is not without challenge at times, especially for the teachers who work directly with students with diverse abilities. "I have had conversations with teachers saying this student shouldn't be at this school," said Caines, "to which I always challenge them, 'Where would you rather have them go?'" For Caines and those on the journey to inclusion, the challenges have been worth it—not only for the students and families that the school reaches now but also for those who come in the future. As Caines explained, "It's not a question of 'if,' but a question of 'when' and 'how many.'"

Inclusion Outcomes

The stories of these schools support special education as part of a strategic vision for a sustainable future for Christian schools. Recent challenges due to the COVID-19 pandemic may have even amplified the potential of special education for long-term sustainability. Sector-level research, conducted during the pandemic, found that enrollment increased by nearly 10 percent in Christian schools that increased special education support and reopened for on-campus instruction, while it decreased by over 20 percent in schools that decreased special education support and reopened with either hybrid or remote instruction.[15]

The benefits of inclusion are not limited to financial sustainability, however. The Flourishing Schools Research initiative from ASCI also uncovers suggestive evidence of improved outcomes for the entire school community. For example, alumni of Christian schools that are responsive to the special needs of students are 50 percent more likely to report they are currently walking with God.[16] And when similar schools (in terms of size, funding, and location) are more responsive to special needs, teachers are more likely to engage in holistic teaching, students are more likely to understand their purpose as part of God's story and report that their teachers exemplify Christlikeness, and parents are more likely to be in a strong partnership with the school.[17]

In his extensive research with youth with disabilities and their families, Erik Carter of Vanderbilt University found that to "be present, invited, welcomed, known, accepted, supported, cared for, befriended, needed, and loved—all were identified by participants as aspects of what it means to be truly included in a community of faith."[18] Although Carter's work is specific to students with disabilities, we believe his work has applicability and provides a compelling model of belonging in Christian schools for all students who fit the school's mission. Ultimately, schools that prioritize the inclusion of underserved students will not only achieve their mission with even greater numbers of students but also will better honor the *imago Dei* in students of all backgrounds and abilities and reflect the diversity of God's good creation.

PART TWO
STRUCTURES AND PRACTICES

CHAPTER FOUR

RESOURCE CREATIVELY

Our God has boundless resources. The only limit is in us. Our asking, our thinking, our praying are too small. Our expectations are too limited.

—A.B. Simpson, founder,
the Christian and Missionary Alliance[1]

Throughout Scripture, God uses various means to provide and care for his people, whether supernaturally (Genesis 22:13-14; Exodus 16:1–17:7), through private goodwill (Exodus 3:22; 12:36), by releasing public resources (1 Kings 10:10; 2 Chronicles 36:22–23; Ezra 1:1–4, 6:1–12), or through the faithful work of God's people serving in influential governmental positions (Genesis 41:25–36). In all of these instances,

God shows himself faithful to provide and to meet the needs of his people. And though the form may appear different, the common theme across these examples is the grateful response of God's people in stewarding these resources to build God's kingdom on earth. Likewise, God uses different means at different times to make provision for Christian schools to fulfill the missions he has entrusted to them.

Historically, most Christian schools have been funded by means of families' tuition and charitable contributions from individuals or organizations. But several schools in our study think more broadly about the kinds of resources that God can make available—and how they can employ those nontraditional resources in faithful pursuit of their missions. As Scott Rodin, author of *The Steward Leader*, explains, "The commitment to be a godly steward comes with a radically new set of lenses. . . . Nothing looks quite the same, and that includes the physical resources at our disposal. Buildings, endowments, land, and other such resources require our best work as stewards. This can result in some pretty unusual actions."[2] The noteworthy actions we explore in this chapter include expansive use of monies from private school choice programs (Valley Christian Schools in Ohio and HOPE Christian Schools in Wisconsin), receipt of other public resources like special education support or auxiliary funds (HOPE Christian Schools, Chattanooga Christian School, and Cincinnati Hills Christian Academy), and entrepreneurship and facility leasing (Lynden Christian Schools in Washington State and Hope Academy in Minnesota).

Private School Choice

By early 2021, seventy-six private school choice programs had been enacted across the United States, with seven new programs and twenty-three expanded programs in 2021 alone.[3] These programs don't merely provide benefits to families and private schools but also represent good fiscal policy: one evaluation of forty private school choice programs through fiscal year 2018 concluded that these programs generated between $12.4 billion and $28.3 billion in taxpayer savings.[4] In this section, we highlight the practices of two schools in our study that have used these programs to sustain their missions and expand accessibility to more families.

Valley Christian Schools (Youngstown, Ohio)

As described in chapter 1, when Valley Christian Schools (VCS) was established in 1975, the founding pastor expressed a desire for the school to serve students of all races and backgrounds across Youngstown. Despite serving predominantly middle-class families for three decades, the school returned to this founding vision in the early 2000s, a return that was enabled by two things: a capital campaign to build a high school and the launch of Ohio's Educational Choice Scholarship Program. "I would say that the EdChoice scholarship was a game changer for access for us," head of school Shelley Murray shared. One teacher echoed Murray's thoughts, commenting that the decision to participate in the EdChoice program "was part of the transformation for our students and our schools. It absolutely contributed to our mission."

In 2022, the school participates in four statewide scholarship programs: both the traditional EdChoice program and the EdChoice Expansion Scholarship, the Jon Peterson Special Needs Scholarship Program, and the Autism Scholarship Program. "We are now 95 percent funded by state scholarships," president Michael Pecchia estimated. For the school, participating in these programs is a way to expand the scope of their mission and to make their schools more accessible to families in the community. But participating in these voucher programs did not merely increase accessibility for general education students. The Peterson Scholarship Program and Autism Scholarship Program in particular have allowed them to provide a more inclusive education, building their special education department, which was founded in 2009. Vice president for school effectiveness and strategic initiatives Joshua Reichard shared, "This is what God provided for us to help serve the people that he wanted to serve and to give access to people who didn't have access before."

Part of the strategy for making the school more accessible included eliminating the requirement of a pastoral referral form, which they had previously used to evaluate prospective families' spiritual lives. Although the school continues to offer a distinctively Christian education, this change meant that families no longer had to identify as Christian. Although conventional wisdom might suggest that such a decision and the related change in student demographics could result in altering their mission, this was not the case for Valley Christian Schools. A peer-reviewed research article by Joshua Reichard concluded that tuition-paying parents and voucher parents were no different in terms of their level of religiosity.[5]

HOPE Christian Schools (Milwaukee, Wisconsin)

Like Valley Christian Schools, HOPE Christian Schools (HOPE) in Milwaukee, Wisconsin are supported by private school scholarships that help make Christian education accessible. The Milwaukee Parental Choice Program is one of the oldest voucher programs in the nation, first launched in 1990. Evaluations of the program find that it positively affected student learning, both for students using vouchers[6] and those remaining in Milwaukee's public schools,[7] while generating $1.6 million in taxpayer savings as early as 1994, rising to $31.9 million in 2008.[8]

Jim Rahn, one of the founders as well as a current board member of Open Sky Education (which oversees the HOPE schools), had a vision for creating a network of Christian schools to serve neighborhoods in urban Milwaukee. Although in 1995, an amendment to the Milwaukee Parental Choice Program first allowed religious schools to participate, the amendment was quickly challenged as a violation of the Establishment Clause. In 1998, in *Jackson v. Benson*, the Wisconsin Supreme Court upheld the expansion, ruling that it did not violate the First Amendment of the United States Constitution. The decision allowed the vision for HOPE to go forward. "Overnight, the vast majority of children in Milwaukee have the opportunity to attend the religious school of their choice," Rahn recalled. Today, HOPE operates a network of six Christian schools in Milwaukee almost entirely funded by the Milwaukee Parental Choice Program, with an additional campus in Racine funded by the Racine Parental Choice Program. Together, these schools make Christian education accessible to over three thousand students in Wisconsin.

There is, of course, a tension between the strategies of relying too much or too little on public resources. Even schools that rely relatively little on public resources still make use of federal programs that provide lunch, health services, or busing for students. All schools are cognizant of the potential threat that public goodwill may expire and withdraw support for the use of public resources for private—and, in particular, faith-based—schools. Recent Supreme Court decisions in cases such as *Trinity Lutheran Church of Columbia, Inc. v. Comer* (2017) and *Espinoza v. Montana Department of Revenue* (2020) suggest that religious liberties remain protected—for now. But for HOPE,

The method of school financing must serve the school's mission, and not the other way around.

ultimately, the voucher program is a means to an end, but not an end in and of itself: the program enabled HOPE to make a "full and lasting education" accessible to as many students as possible, in keeping with their mission. Andrew Neumann, executive chair and CEO of Open Sky Education, rejected "the idea of [not] taking government funding because it could be withdrawn," explaining that Christian schools "might as well provide a Christian education to as many kids as you can for as long as you can." In other words, the method of school financing must serve the school's mission, and not the other way around.

Other Public Resources

One myth worth dispelling is the idea that public resources are exclusively reserved for public schools. By virtue of providing public goods, private schools may rightly be considered public schools in one sense, and entitled to public resources set aside to support their work.[9]

Several federal programs are designed to help families and students who fall into particular demographic groups, regardless of the sector of the school in which they ultimately enroll. In addition to federal funding, private schools may also be eligible for programs run at the state or local level. Three schools in our study in particular demonstrate the ways that these programs can be accessed and leveraged to support their missions, beginning again with HOPE.

HOPE Christian Schools (Milwaukee, Wisconsin)

HOPE utilizes a number of public resources beyond the funds available through private school choice programs. In addition to receiving equitable services from local public school districts because they enroll many students from lower socioeconomic demographics, HOPE receives additional funds and resources through federal Title I, Title II, Title IV, and Individuals with Disabilities Education Act (IDEA) allocations. As part of the Elementary and Secondary Education Act (ESEA) and Every Student Succeeds Act (ESSA) reauthorization, Title I helps provide resources with schools from low-income families, Title II supports effective instruction by supporting professional development, and Title IV provides funds for student-enrichment activities.

According to HOPE's director of federal programs and compliance, "These programs bring counselors into our buildings, coaches for our staff and administrators, to help get them ready for lifelong teaching opportunities." At times, accepting public funds may come with regulatory strings attached, and many schools may prefer autonomy to these additional funds and the compliance they entail.[10] HOPE's director continued, "I would always recommend to any leader who is looking into a new funding stream to connect with other schools that accept that funding to know exactly what the regulatory commitments are." A school may already be in compliance with some new funding streams, for example; in such cases, these public resources represent additional funds with very little human resource investment from the school.

Chattanooga Christian School (Chattanooga, Tennessee)

Not all private school choice programs in the United States are designed for all schools or for all students to participate. Many have eligibility requirements based on family income or public school enrollment in the prior year. Nearly half of all private school choice programs are designed specifically or provide extra funding for special education students.[11] As we briefly mentioned in chapter 3, Chattanooga Christian School (CCS) participates in Tennessee's Individualized Education Account (IEA) program. The IEA program allows families of students with special needs to use their Basic Education Program dollars to attend a local private school they feel would better meet their needs. This funding varies from district to district, but on average it allows about $7,000 in public funds to follow a family to a private school of their choosing.

Importantly, the IEA program allows private schools to charge more than the Basic Education Program allocation for a family to enroll their child.[12] In practice, this means that Chattanooga Christian School families can use the IEA program to pay for additional services through The Learning Center, which costs roughly $7,000 more than general education tuition. This policy allows the school to maintain a sense of tuition equity for general education and The Learning Center students. However, from a policy lens, there is still opportunity for improvement; while the IEA program allows copay, the local public school district retains federal funds allocated to special education students, rather than allowing the money to follow the child to his or her school of choice.

Cincinnati Hills Christian Academy (Cincinnati, Ohio)

The Ohio Department of Education allocates per-pupil auxiliary funds for students enrolled in nonpublic schools, which can be used to reimburse schools for the purchase of educational resources and services. Ohio's Auxiliary Services Program includes secular textbooks, speech and hearing diagnostic or therapeutic services, and standardized testing.[13] In contrast with the possibility of significant regulatory strings attached to participation in private school choice programs, there are few strings attached to these auxiliary funds, and therefore little reason not to use them. "These funds have already been set aside for all students. Private schools just need to know to ask for them," shared Dean Nicholas, head of school at Cincinnati Hills Christian Academy (CHCA). Over the years, the school has used the Auxiliary Services Program to reimburse hundreds of thousands of dollars of purchases, including nearly $130,000 of culinary equipment. This equipment has allowed the school to develop a robust interdisciplinary curriculum, allowing students to earn credits in culinary arts, international studies, and business.

At the federal level, the extension of the Coronavirus Aid, Relief, and Economic Security (CARES) Act provisions to private schools during the COVID-19 pandemic broadened Christian schools' access to, and participation in, these types of auxiliary programs. In summer of 2020, ACSI's survey of member schools during COVID found that the vast majority of schools (83.7 percent) indicated they had received funds through the Paycheck Protection Program of the CARES Act. Close to half of schools (46.2 percent) also reported participation in Equitable Services programs through the CARES Act.[14]

Nonetheless, there are some very real shortcomings to these types of funding sources. While schools like CHCA have discerned ways of accessing public funds intended for the purchase of educational materials, professional development, and special education testing, these processes can and should be more transparent to navigate. Without greater clarity and ease for private schools to obtain these funds, it remains difficult for schools to become aware of and access them. Not only does it make little sense to have funds available but lack the transparency to allow more private schools to access them, but also private schools serve public needs by providing educational services to their communities and states.

Other Revenue Streams

Many of the stories shared thus far are examples of resourcing creatively with the help of public funds and programs. But Christian schools often innovate despite the lack of public support, which is not always available in their states or regions, or may not be aligned with their missions or models. Approaches like entrepreneurship and facility leasing are creative ways that two schools in our study generated third-party revenue streams.

Lynden Christian Schools (Lynden, Washington)

Paul Bootsma, superintendent of Lynden Christian Schools (LCS), explained, "Necessity is the mother of invention. Washington State has a pretty strong separation of private and public. Part of the innovation is finding ways of doing it ourselves. We're rooted in that sort of pioneer spirit." This spirit has been evidenced through the school's long history of entrepreneurship within the community. For example, the oldest building on campus—once used for academic classes—was repurposed into a thrift store. Today, Second Chance Thrift Store is run by a few paid employees augmented by a large staff of community volunteers, many of whom are grandparents or parents of LCS alumni. The thrift store generates a sizeable $500,000 of revenue each year, helping to defray some of the cost of education for many students. In addition, Lynden's growing Career and Technical Education (CTE) programs generate additional revenue streams for the school. For example, plant sale events—featuring plants grown in the working greenhouse on campus—are popular with the community (see photo insert).

Interestingly, not only do these entrepreneurial efforts provide additional revenue for the school, but they also create connections with the surrounding community. When the research team visited Second Chance Thrift Store during a regular school day, it was bustling with community members shopping for clothing, furniture, and household goods. During the visit, the greenhouse tables were covered with holiday wreaths that were labeled for pickup by both school families and others in the community who had ordered them for Christmas. In this small rural town south of the US-Canada border, this school is providing useful goods and services to the community while benefiting the school's financial position and providing educational and vocational training opportunities for its students. In short, the school has developed a win-win approach to entrepreneurship and community engagement that both benefits and goes far beyond the school's bottom line.

Hope Academy (Minneapolis, Minnesota)

Like other schools mentioned in this chapter, Hope Academy was founded with the desire of making Christian education affordable and accessible for more families. This desire is captured in their mission statement: "To foster hope in God within the inner-city neighborhoods of Minneapolis by providing youth with a remarkable, God-centered education." But unlike other schools in this chapter, which rely more heavily on publicly funded private school choice programs, Hope relies heavily on charitable contributions from partners who help make tuition affordable. (Hope's "flipped" financial model—where donors cover up to 90 percent of tuition, and families pay the remainder—is discussed in depth in chapter 1.)

Implementing Hope's vision requires strategic planning and creative use of resources, beyond its innovative funding model to cover student tuition. In addition to this model, Hope manages its property—an expansive 200,000 square foot building in the urban center of Minneapolis—like a cooperative, renting out portions to various nonprofit organizations, including a Teen Challenge ministry. While these organizations pay far less per square foot than they would in other facilities, their rent helps to cover utilities and other physical plant costs. When asked about the viability of this model for other schools seeking to create an income stream from facility leasing, a Hope board member expressed that the potential for such arrangements in urban settings is enormous:

If they're going to be in a low-income neighborhood, there are probably tons of buildings they can get for pennies on the dollar. You get donors that come alongside you to acquire the building, you figure out the financing of it, and then you can get tenants in there. And then you just find other ministries that would partner with you and be willing to pay a lease so that the operating cost of that building is covered, like really keeping the HVAC going and the maintenance and some of those things.

This model of facilities sharing has been replicated across Spreading Hope, a network of schools that originated from Hope Academy, with the same goal of planting affordable urban schools across the country. And in addition to providing income to cover operating expenses, facility leasing has the benefit of turning an often-vacant city building into a hub for a school, community agencies, and parachurch ministries that in turn can bless the larger community in which the building is situated (see photo insert).

The Sustainability Paradox: Funding Impermanence

The various strategies for resourcing creatively that we discuss in this chapter all share a common goal—to increase the accessibility of Christian education. When it comes to public resources—including both private school choice scholarships and auxiliary programs operated at the state level, and programs funded and run at the federal level—Christian schools may understandably be wary of their long-term sustainability. At no point in history have faith-based schools enjoyed an absolute and permanent guarantee that the state would seek their welfare and continuance. But for private schools, *no* income source is ever guaranteed. Philip Scott of ACSI's public policy and legal affairs, in the article "The Other Half of School Choice," makes the argument that "any funding source upon which a school relies requires attention, whether that funding comes from tuition-paying parents, charitable giving, a sponsoring church, and even government-based parental choice programs."[15]

All of these funding sources bear inherent risk in some way and for that reason require that schools protect, plan, and advocate for their continuance. For example, schools regularly create multiyear plans to raise tuition, fully staff development offices to cultivate donor relationships that lead to financial giving and in the case of church-sponsored schools, negotiate relationships and sometimes legal agreements for the use of shared space. Likewise, Scott argues, "Schools should not be scared to consider furthering the mission of a Christian education" through public funding sources, "but they must remember that the more reliant they are on a funding source, the more bound they are to care about that funding source." As explained by Andrew Neumann, "Just like accepting philanthropy to fund a private school, if schools choose to accept public funding, they must also accept the responsibility to advocate on a continuous basis to protect and ideally expand the source of this funding." Perhaps for this reason, many leaders of schools receiving private school choice monies in this study also engage in advocacy work; for example, Neumann has served for close to a decade as the chair of the board for School Choice Wisconsin, currently chairs the School Choice Wisconsin Action board, and is regularly involved both on a state and national level with school choice advocacy.

Although their means may differ—whether using public scholarship programs to completely cover tuition, third revenue streams to defray the cost of tuition, or charitable and strategic partnerships to significantly reduce the cost of tuition—the schools in this study earnestly desire to make their educational programs more accessible to more families, including those who could not otherwise afford a private, faith-based education. This emphasis on accessibility in a discussion on sustainability comes as no surprise, given some of the study's descriptive quantitative findings (see appendix). Accessibility—not only as a component but particularly "supporting underserved students" as an individual item—was one of the strongest and most robust predictors of a respondent's optimism that the school would be both open and more accessible ten years in the future. Historically speaking, innovating new strategies to resource their programs creatively has always been the territory of private schools. The schools in this study have provided ample evidence of this pioneering mindset in Christian schools to continue to innovate and resource creatively, with the goal of making their schools more accessible, sustainable, and future-ready.

CHAPTER FIVE

REIMAGINE STRUCTURES

As we face a very uncertain future, the answer is not to do better what we've done before. We have to do something else. The challenge is not to fix this system but to change it; not to *ref*orm it but to *trans*form it.

—Sir Ken Robinson and Lou Aronica, *Creative Schools*[1]

In their book *Immunity to Change,* Robert Kegan and Lisa Laskow Lahey draw on Ronald Heifetz's work to make a distinction between "technical" and "adaptive" challenges. While technical challenges are those for which routines and processes to solve them are already well known, adaptive challenges are those that are either novel or too complex to apply existing solutions. When faced with adaptive challenges, new ways of thinking about those challenges—from which new solutions can then arise—are needed. According to Kegan and Lahey, not only will most "of the change challenges you face today and will face tomorrow require something more than incorporating new technical skills" but also the "biggest error leaders make is when they apply technical means to solve adaptive challenges."[2]

Multiple authors have outlined the need to shift from technical to adaptive thinking and solutions in various fields, such as Tod Bolsinger in *Canoeing the Mountains*[3] (pertaining to Christian ministry) and Tim Elmore and Andrew McPeak in *Marching Off the Map*[4] (relative to K–12 education). In a convergence of these two fields, the premise for *MindShift: Catalyzing Change in Christian Education* was that "navigating and reframing the complex challenges and opportunities facing our schools" will require "adaptive strategies at both the classroom and school levels."[5] We have outlined the challenges to Christian school sustainability—in terms of enrollment, reach, innovation, and human resources—in the introduction to this book. Taken together, these challenges exceed the current technical skillset available to most schools in the sector.

Creating adaptive (versus technical) solutions requires examining the underlying financial and structural systems at schools. As the late Sir Ken Robinson and coauthor Lou Aronica explain in *Creative Schools*, "If you design a system to do something specific, don't be surprised if it does it. . . . If you want to change education, it's important to recognize what sort of system it is."[6] The systems underlying most private Christian schools—driven by tuition, dependent on donors, and heavy on physical campus costs, often requiring debt and the servicing thereof—are set up in such a way that cost increases often threaten to outpace revenue, educational delivery cannot be scaled, and competitive pay for faculty and staff is perennially out of reach. It is true that a small number of schools with a very affluent clientele and affiliated donor base manage to make these systems work, but often not without sacrificing access and restricting their reach within their communities. And many more schools are prevented from reimagining their underlying structures due to the sunk-cost fallacy, according to which organizations are unwilling to abandon their historical strategies or structures because they are heavily invested in them, even when it is increasingly obvious that abandonment would be better than staying the course.[7]

The majority of schools in our study were opportunity-minded when it came to examining and rethinking their underlying structures, which was part of the criteria for inclusion in the study. Three in particular, however, stood out for the degree to which they transformed these structures in response to adaptive challenges and opportunities. First, two schools in the capital of Pennsylvania joined together to form the Christian School Association of Greater Harrisburg, demonstrating how a district model can provide a pathway to greater health and stability for smaller Christian schools. Next, Oaks Christian School in California was a pioneer in starting an online academy, which has now expanded to serve other Christian schools in helping to meet the growing demand for online education. Finally, in perhaps the most transformational model we have found in the Christian school space, Open Sky Education runs a network of both private Christian schools (HOPE Christian Schools) and public charter schools in multiple states, with plans to expand into new platform-based and microschool delivery models.

Creating adaptive solutions requires examining the underlying financial and structural systems at schools.

A Bridge to Growth: Christian School Districts

While school size is not always a marker for school health, the ability to enroll greater numbers of students is naturally correlated with greater financial resources—and therefore the ability to offer more comprehensive programs, the capacity to pay faculty and staff more competitively, and the funding for capital investments and improvements. By way of contrast, smaller K–12 schools must do the same as larger schools—provide excellent programs, retain qualified teachers to staff those programs, and offer safe and attractive facilities—but with far fewer resources. And yet sector-level data suggests that the majority of Christian schools are small in size, enrolling 240 students or fewer.[8]

In our study, two smaller PK–12 schools—Harrisburg Christian School (HCS, founded in 1955) and West Shore Christian Academy (WSCA, founded in 1973)—came together to create a unified Christian school district in the Capitol District of Harrisburg. In the Christian School Association of Greater Harrisburg (CSAGH) district structure, the schools retain much of their unique identities—everything from branding, sports teams, and tuition structures—but share a statement of faith, centralized administration, and back-office functions. Coming together as an association has enabled more growth and stability than either school could have achieved on its own, through greater purchasing power, an expanded donor base, and increased expertise that has led to better quality of the educational experience—all of which has better positioned the schools for long-term sustainability.

Before CSAGH was founded in January of 2017, Harrisburg Christian School was an independent Christian school on the east side of the Susquehanna River that was collaboration-minded and exploring various merger opportunities with other area schools. In addition, the school had conducted significant fundraising in the hopes of expanding buildings on its existing campus. Across the river on the west side, West Shore Christian Academy was a church-affiliated school that was struggling financially, even though it was located in a growing and more affluent suburb. Because residents on either side of the river seldom cross to the other side, there was little to no competition for students between the two schools (see photo insert). Owing to the difference in the financial positions of the two schools, the transaction was legally an acquisition—HCS acquired WSCA. The head of school at the time, Phil Puleo, explained that "by legal definition, it was an acquisition, but by practice, it was a merger and a collaboration. It was working together for a common purpose." In the months leading up to the acquisition, the two schools and their boards held multiple meetings to build trust. Families that were interconnected between the church and the schools helped to broker this process, as did a focus on the two schools' similar theology and faith commitments. Because of WSCA's tenuous financial situation, the acquisition happened quickly: the agreement was signed on December 27, on January 1 the two schools became one school system, and on January 5 the district transferred all WSCA faculty and staff contracts to new ones at HCS. According to Puleo, "That was a whirlwind of excitement to start the acquisition. But fast-forward to today, CSAGH is operating as a private unified Christian school district and is relatively stable and unified, neither of which has come easily."

Through the district, the two schools have a unified board, shared statement of faith and core vision and mission statements, the same school calendar, and the same policies and handbooks. Operationally, the schools share one superintendent with several district-level employees in a centralized office, which includes finance, fundraising and donor development, and technology. Program-wise, the schools participate together in spiritual emphasis retreats, share most professional development, and have a unified math and science curriculum, with some plans to move forward toward standardizing other curricular areas over time. But as mentioned earlier, some key aspects of the schools remain distinct, including their names, which have not changed since the acquisition. Each school also has its own building principals, and there is little to no student mixing from one campus to the other in terms of enrollment. The schools share some instructional staff, but not many. The two schools also still compete on the athletic field. And in terms of school community and culture, as one board member described, "Parents would say HCS or WSCA. Principals love CSAGH. Faculty see it a bit. But parents and kids have no clue." This approach seems anathema to the more typical approach to mergers; and indeed, other school leaders who had overseen mergers in our study emphasized a need for creating cultural uniformity across campuses. But for CSAGH and the two schools that constitute the district, this has allowed each of the two schools to retain their cultural distinctiveness, thereby enabling them to remain attractive to the communities they already serve.

The benefits of the new district have been many, and have led to greater organizational and financial stability than either school could have hoped to achieve on its own. On the human resources side, both the board and leadership report the value of shared expertise, as well as decreased competition for faculty in a limited talent pool. Financially, the district structure has enabled greater access to funding from Pennsylvania's Education Improvement Tax Credit Program, as well as caught the attention of new donors who are excited about contributing to a unified vision for Christian schooling in the region. And overall, the unification of the two schools—particularly in back-office functions—has provided the impetus and the resources needed to professionalize and implement best practices in finance and administration. As one board member explained, thanks to the district model, "We're able to do things a bit more professionally, and we're able to have resources, both financial and expertise." Another board member expressed that in "going from managing one school to almost doubling in size overnight, it's going from a 'mom and pop' shop to now a company where you need to have standard operating procedures and structures. Where we had two bookkeepers, now we had to hire a CFO. We had to hire a director of HR. We had to do this and do it well, and we had to grow."

While these new (and more expensive) hires meant that some of the board's original hopes around economies of scale did not initially manifest, with better practices in place and an influx of new expertise resulting from the acquisition, the district has now grown to 770 students from seven counties enrolled across both campuses and is in a good cash position. Similar economies of expertise have also been achieved in curricular development, instructional technology, and professional development—all of which are developed and run at the district level by highly qualified staff (versus on an ad hoc basis, at two different schools, by overstretched staff who were not always appropriately trained or resourced). Regarding the district's financial position and the educational experience both schools now offer, board chair Rob Pepper explained, "That's the first time this has happened probably for either of these schools in probably twenty years. So I think sustainability is there. And we're feeling better about the quality of the product."

Bringing two smaller schools into a single district was not without its challenges, and certainly there was no guarantee that doing so would result in both schools finding greater stability together. In fact, conventional wisdom might suggest that there was a greater likelihood of failure than success. However, for HCS and WSCA, going it together versus alone was key to a healthier future. While the board and school leadership did their best to be responsible and diligent throughout the joining of the two schools, they continually affirmed that the difference maker for this successful outcome was God. As Pepper noted, "I would say we're more adequately able to express on earth the kingdom of God will look like long-term, because we've been able to expand the footprint into churches and pockets and communities that were disconnected that now we can connect." Having now successfully made the initial jump to a district model, there is a consensus among the leadership that adding other schools to the district makes sense in the future for two reasons. First, with robust financial structures, procedures, and expertise now in place, the absorption of additional schools into the district will likely achieve even greater economies of scale. And second, there are missional reasons to continue to add schools; as one board member described, "We want to survive, but we also want to thrive. And a piece of that is to open up access and expand opportunities for more students and families who want or need or desire Christian education."

There is hope that CSAGH's district approach can provide a possible road map for the majority of Christian schools, which are also smaller in size, toward greater sustainability. In fact, the district's story has already inspired other smaller schools in the state of Pennsylvania to join together in similar ways. About an hour east of Harrisburg, Alliance Christian School District was formed in 2020 from the joining of Berks Christian School (serving Berks County) and West-Mont Christian Academy Schools (serving Montgomery and Chester Counties). Like the two schools that constitute CSAGH, the two schools in Alliance Christian School District are in the same geographical region but their communities are distinct enough that they typically don't draw from the same population. For this new Christian school district, the CSAGH story demonstrated the possibility of a district approach to Christian schooling that may generate greater efficiencies and productive collaboration, which in turn can lead to better school health. As Pepper explained, "Growth is a byproduct of a healthy school community. You don't grow and then become healthy." In the case of CSAGH, the district structure has provided a bridge for two smaller schools—divided by a river, but united by a shared mission and vision—to increased health for both schools and for Christian schooling within a geographical region.

Going Online: Lessons from a Pioneer

While nearly all Christian schools turned to some form of online instruction during the COVID-19 pandemic, just over half (56 percent) plan to discontinue their distance learning options beyond COVID.[9] This may be due to a lack of staffing or expertise, a steep learning curve to move from emergency distance learning to high-quality offerings, the high costs of additional technology investment, or concerns about undermining existing brick-and-mortar enrollment. However, a third of schools (30 percent) plan to keep current options in place, and another 15 percent plan to expand them in some way. For those schools that perceive online education as an opportunity for reaching more students, one school in our study—Oaks Christian School in Westlake, California—has lessons to share from being a pioneer in this space.

As discussed in chapter 1, in 2011, the school launched Oaks Christian Online, with middle- and high school programs that use both live and independent instruction. The initial desire for launching the program was to offer 100 percent virtual learning for students who needed more flexibility in their learning, including missionary families, international students, and students or parents who are professional artists or athletes. This provided a platform for a fully online degree at one-fourth the cost of the traditional, on-campus degree—thereby expanding Oaks Christian's reach not only beyond its geographical boundaries but also to families for whom a traditional Christian education was financially out of reach. While this 100-percent-virtual learning model continues to serve students in this way, it has expanded since its inception in two key ways. First, it has become a platform for all brick-and-mortar Oaks Christian students to experience learning in an online environment, as leadership reported that most students will take a course through Oaks Christian Online at some point during their time at the school. And second, it has provided a platform to partner with and support other Christian schools across the country. As one administrator expressed, "With a brick-and-mortar school, you're obviously limited to your area. . . . There was a sustainability piece on the financial side, and there was a piece of how do we continue to expand the mission of Oaks Christian beyond our valley here."

As it is currently configured, the online program is 95 percent asynchronous and 5 percent synchronous, with nearly all courses aligning with campus content, particularly in course outcomes and objectives, with adjustments made in pedagogical approaches that reflect best practices in online education. Currently, there are seven hundred students enrolled on Oaks Christian Online; of that number, forty-five are full-time, with about half residing in Southern California and the other half spread throughout the United States and the globe. Initially the school required that students live outside a thirty-mile radius to enroll in the online program, but that was lifted once the school saw that initial fears of the online program "cannibalizing" the on-campus student body proved to be unfounded. The online option provides not only greater flexibility for students who need it but also a Christian education that is far more affordable for those for whom the on-campus sticker price is too high. Although the online diploma costs about a fourth of the traditional brick-and-mortar version ($9,000 annually versus $36,000 annually), it has its own diploma and students in the program cannot participate in any on-campus offerings (such as athletics and arts and music). According to an administrator, this has provided access to an Oaks Christian education for middle-class families in particular who cannot afford the on-campus price tag. Admission to the program is also not as rigorous or competitive as the brick-and-mortar program. Although the online program has been available for ten years, leaders report that only now is the program transitioning from being a cost center to turning a profit, due to the significant financial and technological investment required to start an online program. The lag time to profitability was not unexpected, however; as one administrator explained, "We made the investment because we anticipated that over the course of time it would continue to grow."

In part because of their own experiences with investing in online education, and also to expand the reach of their program, Oaks Christian now partners with other schools to help them bring online courses to their students. As a school administrator shared, "We allowed the program to evolve . . . recognizing that an online program was a need, and other schools probably needed the same thing. So let's go out and find schools where we can offer them our online program to help supplement their own." Oaks Christian currently partners with ten Christian schools to deliver online education, many of which are in Southern California, but also in other parts of California and as far away as Florida, Georgia, and New York. There is a wide diversity in how partner schools utilize Oaks Christian's courses, often supplementing or enriching their course catalogs with classes they do not or cannot offer. Some elementary schools looking to expand into middle school will even use the program to offer the bulk of courses, beyond what they can provide by adding a section to a current teacher's course load. According to this administrator, the addition of the online program thus allows some schools to expand their offerings quickly, while avoiding "all of the capital investments of salaries and buildings and all these different components." As the administrator explained, the partnership program has allowed Oaks Christian to become "a support to Christian schools as well, who don't have an online program or have the resources of Oaks Christian to be able to put that together."

Given the tremendous potential market for online Christian education, and the possibilities for enriching existing brick-and-mortar programs through supplemental online courses, online education is worth considering as a delivery model for the sector. However, Oaks Christian's story suggests that developing an entirely new online education program is likely not possible for many individual Christian schools, given the required investment. As one administrator at the school described,

> I would say in most cases, starting your own online program is probably not the answer for most schools. . . . You have to have the right people. You have to have the right processes in place, which includes the systems. And then you have to have the right product. Those are the three key foundational pieces you need to have in place to be successful, and all of them take time and money. And if you don't have the resources to be able to support all of them, then it's not going to work.

This reality may have been driven home all the more during the COVID-19 pandemic, and may explain why a majority of Christian schools plan to discontinue distance learning afterward. As one Oaks Christian administrator posited, "The biggest thing that people are recognizing after having tried to do remote learning, which is very different from online learning, is it's not easy. It does require a lot of effort and it actually is a lot more expensive than people really realize." Despite these difficulties on the delivery side, however, online education is still an option that more and more parents are choosing, especially during the pandemic; for example, from 2019 to 2020, enrollment in online charter schools across the country grew significantly, including in Pennsylvania where the number of online students jumped by 59 percent.[10] In considering the future opportunities of online Christian education, creating new online programs offers well-resourced schools like Oaks Christian a way to expand the school's reach and add another revenue stream. Oaks Christian's experience—that offering an online program did not cannibalize their brick-and-mortar program—is consistent with empirical research suggesting that students enrolling in online programs seek a distinctive experience from those who enroll in person.[11] For those individual schools that cannot afford the development process and long horizon needed to build a successful program, however, it will be essential to partner with other schools, networks, organizations, or other kinds of providers in order to realize the promise of expanding their reach through online education.

Networks: Educating Missionally, at Scale

In the preceding chapter, we detail the origin story for HOPE Christian Schools (HOPE). The first HOPE Christian school was founded in Milwaukee in 2002 as a grades 1–4 school that accepted vouchers from the Milwaukee Parental Choice Program. Today, HOPE operates seven K–8 schools in Wisconsin serving approximately thirty-five hundred students, with expansion plans for at least three campuses in the near future. As mentioned, however, HOPE is part of a larger organization known as Open Sky Education, which has leveraged a network approach to deliver accessible education in multiple forms beyond HOPE Christian Schools. These include four open admission, public charter schools (EAGLE College Preparatory Schools) in Arizona, which also offer faith-based wraparound care in the form of before- and after-school care and preschool programming provided by Compass Educational Programs. In addition, Open Sky's Character Formation Project is embedded within each campus, with civic curriculum for the public charter schools and Christian curriculum for the Compass programs.

HOPE's founders believed that a full and lasting education was built on three pillars—excellent academics, character formation, and, if families chose it, faith formation—and were determined that this education should be accessible and affordable for all, regardless of geography or socioeconomic status. The founding board took the word "all" very seriously. Jim Rahn, cofounder and board chair of Open Sky, described an early and pivotal board meeting:

> A number of our board members said, "The day we stop talking about expansion is the day I quit." And we've never looked back from that day. We've never set out to create the best single site school in America. We want to operate the most effective schools, plural. There's a big difference between those, because plural means you have to have things that can scale systems, that scale financial independence.

This commitment gave birth to the idea that networks are a structural way to scale educational delivery. According to Andrew Neumann, Open Sky's executive chair and CEO, "The whole idea is to set our structure up to serve our mission, as opposed to the other way around. We don't want the mission to serve our structure" (see photo insert).

For this reason, Open Sky has created a number of structural innovations that undergird its ability to run multiple networks of not only schools but also educational programs to serve those schools. One of these innovations is its legal and governance structure, which is better described as a network of nonprofits. Open Sky serves as the parent nonprofit, with forty staff who launch and manage schools, as well as make centralized decisions around curricula and programs.

Beneath this parent nonprofit, each network of schools in each state is their own nonprofit corporation, with a legal agreement between the Open Sky board and each nonprofit board under it. Then under each regional nonprofit school organization, every school operates individually as a limited liability corporation (LLC). Separate from this entire structure, but reporting directly up to the parent organization, is Open Sky's nonprofit facilities organization, which acquires, maintains, and manages properties and facilities via leases with each individual school LLC. Legal agreements between all nonprofits and LLCs are carefully crafted to accommodate the diversity of state and local requirements, including managing separations from church and state.

As Neumann explained, "The architecture is absolutely essential for our ability to do this." This is for a number of reasons, and not just liability protection. The separation of the facilities organization from school operations allows for multi-tenant buildings and, in the case of the public charter schools, separate faith-based tenants unaffiliated with the schools that can provide wraparound and related services. Having experts in real estate and building management actually running the facilities side also creates efficiencies that often can elude school leaders, who are not necessarily skilled in those areas. But perhaps most importantly from a financial perspective, the facilities organization is able to pool the lease revenue from the various schools and other tenants, which helps to ensure that the expenses of a single site—such as a new roof, or start-up costs—is offset and does not affect educational delivery at that site. Neumann explained, "The cost of real estate could be a major fluctuation in the type of education we can afford to give to children. By pooling facilities expenses, we charge the schools all the same portion of their revenue for rent. So every single child gets an equal amount of remaining resources for the education, allowing for equity in the educational programming we can provide across all campuses regardless of the fluctuation in facility costs from campus to campus." When coupled with policies around strict budgeting and cash reserve metrics, these structures create not only financial stability but also the margin for expanding networks. Rahn observed that "without margin, there is no mission. You cannot be entrepreneurial and grow a business of any kind if you're in a constant state of dependency. And the quickest way to become dependent is to be upside down financially."

In turn, Open Sky's structures have enabled them to develop new educational networks and models to meet new opportunities. Neumann explained that although HOPE Christian Schools started when "Milwaukee was the epicenter of vouchers in our country, then we ran out of growth room—we couldn't go to other states with that model, because there weren't other states that had a prolific enough funding model for vouchers." In turn, Open Sky considered how to move into states with new charter opportunities, while offering accompanying faith-based afterschool programs. Back in the early 2000s with the charter school movement more established and regulated, Open Sky was turning its attention to new areas of opportunity and new models that may be birthed to meet them. As Rahn shared, Open Sky's leadership is continuously challenging itself by asking, "Is the mission of Open Sky to build brick-and-mortar schools at specific locations and create schools that look like schools always have, or is our mission really the three C's—Christ, Character, and College, which has been our shorthand for the mission? And if that's true, then what are the ways in which we might be able to expand that reach and additionally connect children and families in a lifelong relationship with Jesus Christ?"

This question has most recently led to planning for a new technology-enabled microschool model, that will be smaller in size than Open Sky's current schools (of four hundred to six hundred students), can be operated anywhere geographically, and feature instructional innovations around personalized learning and multi-aged groupings. According to Neumann:

> This model will meet the demand of middle America.
> Those with the lowest income in certain areas have access

to vouchers and tax credits. The top percentage, a very small group of people, can afford the traditional cost of a private faith-based education. Then there's a large group in America, the middle 80 or 90 percent, that's left out. And we've got to figure this out—back to our mission of a full and lasting education, that is affordable and accessible to all. There are just not enough options that are affordable and accessible to them. We want to create a new option.

With this new "platform" model on the horizon, Open Sky continues to live up to its name by innovating structurally to meet opportunities for achieving its mission with even more students. Ultimately, according to Neumann, a diversity of educational models is the goal: "We want the ecosystem of educational options that exist for kids to be just as diverse as the ecosystem of children it's meant to serve." This is in stark contrast to the traditional approach in the Christian school sector—with leaders looking for the best ways to improve on a single model of schooling, without questioning the dominance of the model itself. The Open Sky story provides evidence that, as Tom Vander Ark and Lydia Dobyns write in their book about school networks titled *Better Together*, "as dynamic networks with powerful platform tools create a network effect, they get better and more valuable as they grow. . . . Platforms change assumptions about what is possible, and they unlock new sources of value creation and supply."[12] In this sense, Open Sky's network approach provides one of the most transformational models of schooling in the study, and indeed that can be found in the Christian education sector.

From Tinkering to Transformation

A Christian school district, online academy, and networks of schools are examples of reimagined structures for Christian education we found in our study and explored in this chapter, but they are not the only ones emerging in the sector. Other examples include completely online Christian schools, homeschool partnerships and learning pods, microschools, and University-Model® Schools (UMS), to name a few.[13] Recent research on hybrid schools in the United States suggests that not only are these schools opening at an increasing rate but also the majority are faith-based. Further, with an average annual tuition of $4,158, hybrid schools are more affordable than most traditional private schools—suggesting that many of these schools offer an affordable and flexible option for families who are seeking Christian education but who have not been able to access traditional Christian schools because of cost.[14]

While not part of the sample for our study because their structural innovation began in 2020, Second Baptist School in Houston, Texas, is an example of the recent and rapid growth in hybrid models for Christian schools. In 2020, the leadership began to realize its vision of extending Christian education to the greater Houston area, as head of school Don Davis shared: "We dreamed about offering quality Christian education to more families and what an alternative school model could look like." As a ministry of Second Baptist Church under the leadership of senior pastor Ed Young, the school decided that Paratus Classical Academy was the school model that most closely aligned with their mission and vision for Christian education. Paratus was a classical UMS founded by Second Baptist School graduate Beau Dollins and his wife Pam, where students attended on-campus classes two or three days per week, with the other days spent learning via satellite and studying under the supervision of parents guided by the school program.

When Paratus joined SBS in 2020, the leadership immediately began replication of the classical UMS model, with three sites launching on Second Baptist Church campuses in the 2021–2022 school year. This expanded the Paratus student enrollment of two hundred students to more than five hundred students enrolled across the classical UMS sites. Davis explained that Second Baptist School's new model "allows for Christian education to be accessible to more families who either had a financial need or a desire to serve as co-educators in the school experience."

In 2023–2024, Second Baptist School will open two additional sites, with a projected enrollment total of twenty-five hundred students across all six campuses—more than doubling the school's total system enrollment in just three years. This exponential growth reflects the strength of like-minded Christian schools coming together to achieve a greater vision. When asked about the unusual arrangement of a traditional Christian school partnering with a classical UMS, Davis shared, "The educational structure of each model looks different, but both are aligned to fulfill a unified mission and vision. While our schedules and curriculum may differ, we share the same goals—to provide a Christ-centered education that is academically excellent within a caring community. In a united effort, we accomplish more for the kingdom together than we would separately."

As evidenced in the case of Second Baptist School's hybrid model and in the schools in our study, Christian schools are reexamining and transforming the fundamental models by which they deliver on their educational missions, and not just tinkering around the edges of their existing models by making technical tweaks. This is a hopeful development not just for individual schools but also for the future of the Christian school sector; as Sir Ken Robinson and Lou Aronica explain, "Systems as a whole are capable of changing too, and in many ways they already are. The more innovation there is within them, the more likely they are to evolve as a whole."[15] All of these innovative examples suggest that the Christian school sector—and with it, Christian schools of all backgrounds and profiles—can rise to meet adaptive challenges to sustainability with transformational solutions, and in turn ensure their missions continue into the future.

Christian schools are reexamining and transforming the fundamental models by which they deliver on their educational missions, and not just tinkering around the edges of their existing models by making technical tweaks.

Chattanooga Christian School in Tennessee allocates resources in a deliberate way that has allowed them to strategically invest in people instead of buildings. For example, the school has never incurred any debt to build out its fifty-five-acre campus at the base of Lookout Mountain. Instead, the school has maximized the use of re-engineered metal buildings and employed design techniques like color blocking and abundant landscaping to enhance the cutting-edge aesthetic of the campus. Head of school Chad Dirkse refers to the buildings as flexible "grow spaces, not show places."

What began as a modest, student-run coffee cart ten years ago at **Cincinnati Hills Christian Academy** is now a student-run coffee bar that serves ethically sourced coffee and grosses $50,000 per year. The business also gave rise to the school's Entrepreneurship and Sustainability Program, which incubates business ventures such as a greenhouse and teaching kitchen that sells student-made products to community members. This robust initiative combines innovation, real-life learning, leadership development, business and management skills, and environmental-sustainability goals in an effort not only to train student leaders but also to connect with and serve the local community.

The **Christian School Association of Greater Harrisburg** was formed in 2017, when Harrisburg Christian School (founded in 1955) acquired West Shore Christian Academy (founded in 1973) to create a unified Christian school district in the capital region of Pennsylvania. The two schools remain distinct entities in different communities that are located on opposite sides of the Susquehanna River (pictured). The district structure has provided a metaphorical bridge of its own for two smaller schools—divided by a river but united by a shared mission and vision—to achieve greater financial stability, and demonstrates the potential for such districts to lead to greater health for individual schools as well as Christian schooling within a geographical region.

At **The City School** in Philadelphia, head of school Joel Gaines (pictured) emphasizes the ways in which partnering and sharing resources with local churches, ministries, businesses, and organizations enables the school and the community to accomplish exponentially more—"to go far" together, in the words of the African proverb that graces the student-created mural at the upper-school campus.

Hope Academy manages its property—an expansive 230,000-square-foot building in the urban center of Minneapolis—like a cooperative, renting out portions to like-minded nonprofits. While these organizations pay far less per square foot than they would in other facilities, their rent helps to cover utilities and other physical plant costs. This model of facilities sharing has been replicated across Spreading Hope, a network of schools that originated from Hope Academy, with the same goal of planting affordable urban schools across the country. Facilities leasing also has the benefit of turning a vacant city building into a hub for a school, community agencies, and parachurch ministries that in turn can bless the larger community in which the building is situated.

*Students at **Lynden Christian Schools** prepare for their annual plant sale. Many of the school's programs and events like this provide useful goods and services to the rural community in northern Washington state, while benefiting the school's financial position and providing educational and vocational training opportunities for its students. The school has developed a missional, win-win approach to entrepreneurship and community engagement that both benefits and goes far beyond the school's bottom line.*

*The Iroquois Campus of **Grand Rapids Christian Schools** was built on the site of a former public high school in a historic neighborhood that had served the community since 1925. The fact that many of the residents of the neighborhood attended that high school gave a high degree of local attachment to the site. A two-story stained-glass window in the new building depicts the connections between the former school with the community. Other design choices similarly reflect the school leadership's value of their neighbors and the relevance of the school's mission to the community.*

School Will Welcome All Races and Creed

NEARING DEADLINE — Volunteer workers swarm in and out of Youngstown's newest private school located in the former Bancroft School, Wychwood Avenue, as the Sept. 3 opening of the Youngstown Christian School nears. Four to 20 men and women may be found hard at work from dawn until after midnight every day. Smiling as they "paint for the Lord" are, left to right: Mrs. Emily Harasyn, Mrs. Mary Szekel and Mrs. Edie Huba, all members of the congregation of Highway Tabernacle Assemblies of God Church.

ALL SET — Kindergarte Johnny Stephens is excited he answers questions direc to him by Mrs. Carol Ra say, principal of the Your t o w n Christian Sch Enrolling him are his p ents, Mr. and Mrs. J Stephens, 1940 Pointview

HELPFUL STAFF—Mrs. Linda Clacko, who will teach second and third graders, previews new books in the school library with Silke Huba who is transferring from Frank Ohl Middle School in Austintown to the sixth grade at Youngstown Christian School, and Heidi Lunsford, a second grader, who attended Sheridan School last year.

Valley Christian Schools was founded as Youngstown Christian School by the Highway Tabernacle Assembly of God in 1975. The founding pastor of the church was interviewed in a local newspaper article at the time (pictured above) and shared a vision for students of all racial, ethnic, socioeconomic, and church backgrounds coming together to learn at a Christian school in the city. While the following three decades saw enrollment from predominantly middle-class, white students, the founding pastor's vision was achieved in the early 2000s with the opening of a new high school building at which inner-city students from Ohio's Educational Choice Scholarship Program enrolled.

Oaks Christian School in Westlake Village, California, purchased a former pet food facility that became their ten-thousand-square-foot innovation space, called the IDEA (Innovation, Design, Engineering and Aeronautics) Lab, which is now a state-of-the-art fabrication and production facility filled with tools for electric cars (pictured), robotics, aeronautics, and rocketry. Partnerships between industry leaders and over 350 students who work in the IDEA Lab are sparking innovation that enhances relevance for students' learning and for what the school can contribute to the community.

Open Sky Education's Executive Chair and CEO Andrew Neumann *(fourth from left) helps cut the ribbon for a new public, open-admission charter school, EAGLE College Preparatory School, in Arizona. School openings are a common occurrence for Open Sky, which has leveraged a network approach and school choice funding to increase accessibility to quality education. In addition to multiple public charter schools in Arizona, Open Sky also runs HOPE Christian Schools, faith-based wraparound before- and after-school care and preschool programs, and character formation projects for both public and private schools. In keeping with their mission to reach as many children as possible with a "full and lasting" education, Open Sky has added a school and business support arm and is also stepping into the microschool space.*

Partnerships with industry and businesses can enhance student learning and preparation, not only by providing access to necessary equipment and resources, but also by giving students real-life experience and connections with professionals in various fields. At **Valor Christian High School** in Colorado, space was set aside in the new Center for Culture and Influence for a small but centrally located art gallery, where local artists are invited to display their work—which in turn creates an entrée for artists to participate in the center's various other programs and collaborate with Valor students.

CHAPTER SIX

TAKE DISCIPLINED RISKS

A risk is a risk... If risks always paid off, they wouldn't be risks. The promise of stretching is not success, it's learning.

—Chip and Dan Heath, *The Power of Moments*[1]

In the education sector's rush to innovate in recent years, schools might have oversold risk, failing forward, and failure in general. Taking risks does not ensure success, nor does it ensure learning. Repeated, haphazard failure without reflection results in wasted resources—both human and material. Individuals only learn by reflecting on the risks they have taken and learning from the outcome. Likewise, organizations operate in a continuous cycle of reflection, risk, rejection, and revision.[2]

Because risks are real and resources are scarce, before school leaders take risks, they have to count the cost of the risk. Adam Grant, an organizational psychologist at the University of Pennsylvania, has found that successful entrepreneurs are not actually unbridled, risk-taking mavericks. Rather, successful entrepreneurs minimize risk.[3] But schools also have to count the cost of the status quo, a cost that is often overlooked. The risks of not adapting or changing to current and future educational conditions are real and can compromise the mission of Christian schools, both in the short- and long-term. The way forward through this double jeopardy (involving the risks of innovating, but also the risks of staying the same) is often through *disciplined* risk. And adaptive challenges in particular—like the challenges Christian schools face to sustainability—by nature require disciplined risk-taking to find solutions.[4]

Leaders who promote disciplined risk weigh the opportunity cost of maintaining the status quo versus change against their organization's clear mission and vision of their schools. This enables leaders to avoid the fallacy of the status quo being low risk and thoughtfully moving forward with risks that are well-aligned with the school mission. In this chapter, we highlight schools in the study that are doing just this. Even though the risks they have taken have not necessarily felt disciplined to all school constituencies involved, the leaders of these schools have been

> *Leaders who promote disciplined risk weigh the opportunity cost of maintaining the status quo versus change against their organization's clear mission and vision of their schools.*

disciplined in their risk-taking through actions that are (1) *intentional,* meaning risks are gauged by the school's mission rather than driven by fads; (2) *incremental,* meaning risks are taken in small steps so that changes can be progressed or abandoned based on proof of concept; and (3) *iterative,* meaning risk is continually evaluated and ongoing feedback is used by leaders for organizational learning.

Disciplined Risks Are *Intentional*

While "shiny objects" (like new STEM facilities, maker spaces, and the like) are often beneficial to student learning and success, there is no end to the bells and whistles that schools could add to their programs and campuses. Christian schools are not impervious to this temptation and could easily expend much of their resources and staff energy in pursuit of the latest and greatest facility, program, or pedagogy. By way of contrast, the schools in our study approached innovation through the tactic of disciplined risk, specifically by gauging every risk by the yardstick of the school's mission. While chapter 1 provided an in-depth discussion of the importance of mission-mindedness to the sustainability of Christian education, in this section we build on this foundation to show how a laser focus on the mission actually enabled two schools in our study to risk—and innovate—wisely.

Oaks Christian School (Westlake Village, California)

Oaks Christian School feels like a small college campus with an Olympic-sized swimming pool at its center surrounded by athletic, academic, and dormitory complexes spreading over rolling hills. There is an enormous innovation space, the IDEA (Innovation, Design, Engineering and Aeronautics) Lab, filled with tools for robotics, electric cars, aeronautics, and rocketry. Hollywood songwriters, actors, and producers teach some of the school's music, arts, and theater classes. Located just outside of Los Angeles and Malibu, Oaks Christian seems like the kind of place that might fall victim to shiny object syndrome. But as shared in chapter 1, Oaks Christian has a clear focus on its mission after a period of reexamining and reestablishing that mission about ten years ago. Recalling that Oaks Christian's mission statement is "to dedicate ourselves to Christ in the pursuit of academic excellence, artistic expression, and athletic distinction while growing in knowledge and wisdom through God's abundant grace," student learning and development are the guideposts by which innovational risks are assessed.

For example, the English Department chair captured Oaks Christian's approach to disciplined risk-taking: "Our administrators have always asked, 'What do you want to do to inspire kids to be all that they are made to be?' Part of innovation is not jumping on the shiny new thing. It is the freedom to constantly adapt to best meet the needs of the students in front of you. We do not innovate for innovation's sake." As evidence, the department chair shared that they have "said no to a lot of technology" like online books and texts. Rather, the "technology we need is a pen and paper." As the department chair pointed out, the school's focus is on inspiring students to be all they were created to be, not on the tools that might make that possible.

Practically speaking, this means that if a class where students are composing music needs a state-of-the-art studio with keyboards, headphones, and monitors, Oaks Christian finds resources to make that happen. If English teachers want students to use books, paper, and pens to annotate and assess learning, then that is what they provide. In the IDEA Lab, a space filled with what could be many shiny objects collecting dust, the programs flourish because student interest has driven their development and growth. While the IDEA Lab started with around 100 students, by year three, over 350 students were working in the lab and developing courses that integrate art, engineering, and facial recognition software. Student learning needs—which are at the core of Oaks Christian's mission—are what drive the decision-making around risk and innovation.

Many of the school's facilities and programs could be seen as shiny objects that are great photo opportunities for shallow marketing materials. What makes the opportunities substantive, however, is their alignment with Oaks Christian's core mission and the fact that every risk is viewed through that lens. A senior academic dean, in describing how Oaks Christian continues to innovate without chasing innovation for innovation's sake, offered this advice: "Decide what cannot change before you start innovating." Maintaining the core of the mission and finding better ways to deliver the mission is at the heart of Oaks Christian's intentional approach to risk-taking.

The City School (Philadelphia, Philadelphia)

Also discussed in chapter 1, The City School is the result of multiple school mergers. Spruce Hill Christian School and City Center Academy merged in December 2006 and in 2013 were together renamed The City School. In 2014, Philadelphia Mennonite High School merged with The City School, which provided an additional elementary campus and increased impetus to identify a dedicated upper school space. This final step was achieved in 2018, with the opening of the grades 6–12 Poplar Campus. Several leaders and board members described how while the mergers and building changes often felt very risky at the time, each was accomplished through careful planning, multistep rollouts, and continual prayer.

The merger between The City School and Philadelphia Mennonite High School posed a unique set of risks beyond those typical to mergers (e.g., financial, facilities-related, curricular, scheduling, staff), because the two schools were rooted in different denominational backgrounds (Presbyterian and Anabaptist, respectively). As shared in chapter 1, the Reverend Leonard Dow, a board member both then and now, described how passages of Scripture on the "ministry of reconciliation, and the concept of *shalom*, became a common space where we could leave some of the things that tend to divide us denominationally." The merger across distinct denominations became possible once there was agreement on a core, shared mission. One school leader who was present at the time of this merger explained, "We have adhered to our mission through mergers and leadership change. Those who are interested and invested in the school see that we are adhering to our mission." Another leader who was present at the merger added, "There was definitely a concern about losing identity [but also] understanding why God aligned these two schools—we were so similar, especially on service and peacemaking. Once you start to see how they are intertwined you began to see this as the same, just bigger and with more resources."

With this focus on shared mission, the leadership of both schools were able to embark intentionally on a careful process of planning out and implementing the merger. The regional accreditation teams at the time noted the discipline and diligence with which the merger was carried out, as well as the extraordinary feat of merging two schools from very different denominations. Today, while still merged under the umbrella of The City School, there are three campuses in distinctly different neighborhoods in Philadelphia that extend the school's reach and extend its donor base. The City School hopes to establish more elementary schools around the city to feed the upper school campus, with its five core commitments—to Jesus, to *shalom*, to the city, to excellence, and to accessibility—there to guide decision-making and risk-taking in the future.

Disciplined Risks are *Incremental*

Tom DeJonge, head of Grand Rapids Christian Schools, said, "Schools are not well-resourced enough—no matter how well-resourced they are—to start things at random." This was true across all eleven sites in our study, but for two schools in particular, one way to ensure they do not start things at random is to begin with small, calculated risks. In turn, this incremental approach to change has led to the development of new models for sustainability.

Chattanooga Christian School (Chattanooga, Tennessee)

Chattanooga Christian School (CCS) opened in 1970 in a converted Chevrolet car dealership. The school now serves over fourteen hundred students on its main campus. They have never incurred any debt to build out their fifty-five-acre campus at the base of Lookout Mountain by maximizing the use of reengineered metal buildings. Every space is optimized for student use to the point that the head of school, Chad Dirkse, does not have an office of his own so that there is more room for student learning space. As described in chapter 2, because CCS has maintained a strong financial position through disciplined facility use, they have been able to pursue satellite campuses by partnering with local churches in different parts of the city that CCS had previously not been able to reach.

Instead of building new campuses, CCS works with churches to repurpose and renovate spaces for their microschools. The school raises the money to support the projects at the local churches, provides marketing and back-office support, and runs the microschools by hiring staff and supplying curriculum and learning resources. When the school embarked on the process to start microschools, leaders held 150 meetings with pastors and community leaders to find the partners who were willing to partner and share the risk with them. The first microschool, The King School, is a K–5 campus located on the campus of Olivet Baptist Church—a historic church that was a vital part of the civil rights movement in Chattanooga. Purpose Point is a health care center and early childhood center, which is located on the campus of Mount Canaan Church, which operates out of an open-span building that is a converted Kmart. And finally, the K–5 Glenwood School is located on the campus of New City Fellowship located east of downtown Chattanooga.

In keeping with their commitment to disciplined risk, school leaders have launched the campuses in waves. The King School launched in 2019, and Purpose Point and The Glenwood School did not open until 2021. By renovating existing facilities and raising the funds up-front, the school minimized their exposure to risk and ensured that a specific site could be closed if it failed to be financially viable. And ongoing risk is mitigated because the individual microschools are able to keep costs down due to the support they receive from CCS and the reduced costs for facility use they achieve through partnerships with local churches. Overall, this incremental approach to extending the school's reach through microschools has mitigated risk throughout—from initial partnering with community members and churches, to establishing the schools, to running the schools on a daily basis.

Cincinnati Hills Christian Academy (Cincinnati, Ohio)

Also described in chapter 2, Cincinnati Hills Christian Academy (CHCA) illustrates how to incubate incremental risks by constantly learning from productive failure. After investing heavily in an advanced computing lab, CHCA administration observed that teachers and students were not using the space. School leaders realized that innovations were more likely to succeed if the ideas came from teachers, so the school established an innovation fund for teachers. Teachers can apply for funding to support an idea that they would like to implement with students—ideas that range from entrepreneurship efforts to flexible classroom seating. If the proposal is approved by a team of teachers and administrators, then the teacher receives the funding. Most of these innovative ideas are incremental changes to particular areas of the school, but teachers own the ideas and drive the work forward in ways that are meaningful for them and their students.

Similarly, for students, CHCA incubates incremental risk through its entrepreneurship programs. This incubation is how the Leaning Eagle coffee cart business has grown from $15,000 to $50,000 in sales and a fully functioning café at the heart of campus. Each year, through the school's entrepreneurship program overseen by the school's director of entrepreneurship and sustainability, students are able to build on the successes and learn from the failures of ventures from the previous year. Students conduct market research, source products, develop apps, and build business plans. Importantly, some of those plans fail. For example, after the success of the coffee cart that became a café, students were convinced that a smoothie stand would also be successful. However, due to the location of the stand, challenges with getting products, and the limited appeal of smoothies at different times of the day, the smoothie stand failed. Students moved on to a new idea the following year while keeping the café as a profit generator to fund future endeavors.

Eventually, through the incremental growth of entrepreneurial ventures, CHCA now has a greenhouse where students experiment with hydroponics and aeroponics to grow organic vegetables as part of Eagle Farms. A professional teaching kitchen also produces and sells wood-oven pizzas every Friday to the community. Students are generating revenue by selling organic produce from the campus greenhouse. What started as a passion project of a teacher and a few students has grown incrementally, over time, to become a vehicle for learning about science, business, marketing, app creation, fundraising, and developing partnerships in the community.

Disciplined Risks are *Iterative*

Part of this disciplined risk-taking is iterating ideas. While serving as the head of school at Valor Christian High School, Kurt Unruh explained that he and his team often "cluttered the cutting room floor" with ideas they abandoned. As is the habit of great filmmakers, innovative leaders cut many good ideas to make space for even better ideas—a form of disciplined risk-taking. Two schools in particular in our study showed a willingness to iterate in their structures and programs, in a way that not only mitigated risk but also created new opportunities for missional reach and financial sustainability.

HOPE Christian Schools (Milwaukee, Wisconsin)

As we've discussed in preceding chapters, Open Sky Education is the second largest education provider in Milwaukee, Wisconsin—second only to Milwaukee Public Schools. They serve more than thirty-five hundred students on seven campuses through HOPE Christian Schools—one of the highest performing K–8 network of schools in Milwaukee. Because HOPE's ongoing operations are 100 percent funded by Milwaukee Parental Choice Program vouchers and other sources of public funding, underserved students are able to access affordable education in a safe, Christian environment. Each year, Open Sky is able to put 2.5 percent of their revenue into a reserve fund that allows them to absorb significant and unexpected expenses, as well as to invest in improvements or new growth opportunities, without being dependent on philanthropy or incurring debt.

Open Sky has consistently demonstrated how to take disciplined risks including making the hard decision of closing schools. Because of the additional cost to educate high school students coupled with the inadequate additional funding for high school students in the voucher program, over the next year, HOPE will close their high school and reopen it as a K–8 school (along with opening two additional K–8 sites in the city). HOPE has determined, based on their mission and funding model, that at this time K–8 education is the best way to serve the most students in Milwaukee and have the broadest impact on children within the community. In this sense, they have iterated their model until they determined the best approach to achieving their mission. At the same time, HOPE leaders report they are also working closely with school choice advocates and elected leaders to stress the urgent need for increasing funding for high schools in the voucher program, in the hope that over the next few years improved funding will lead to thousands of new fully funded Christian high school seats in Milwaukee and across the state. Thus HOPE is still taking risks in terms of opening new schools, but this iterative process has both mitigated risk and created new opportunities for reach and impact.

Lynden Christian Schools (Lynden, Washington)

As mentioned in chapter 2, up until recently Lynden Christian Schools (LCS) maintained a long-standing recycling program. Like the school's thriving Second Chance Thrift Store, the recycling center was staffed mostly by volunteers from the school community. However, when the program lost its financial viability due to decreased market demand for recycled materials, school leadership decided to shutter the recycling center. School leaders reported this was a difficult loss for community members who highly valued the center and its programs. The decision was not taken lightly, but it was necessary. Currently, the school is developing plans for the new space—possibly to expand into sales of construction materials or to provide a multi-use space for the school's growing Career and Technical Education (CTE) programs, which themselves generate additional revenue streams, such as through the sales of plants grown in the working greenhouse on campus.

LCS's example demonstrates the importance of being willing to let go of programs and approaches that are no longer working, even though there has been a significant sunk cost in the past (in terms of finances, but also people, community involvement, and reputation). Often, schools' unwillingness to stop doing something because of the sunk cost not only keeps failing strategies in place but also creates a secondary cost—an opportunity cost—when energy and resources are tied up and cannot be reinvested in new strategies. In contrast, LCS's iterative approach to buildings and programs helps to create new opportunities for revenue, community engagement, and student learning, which contribute to long-term sustainability into the future.

Disciplined Risk: Overcoming "Change as Loss"

All of the schools in our study experienced significant changes in their financial models and organizational structures, although those changes differed from school to school. Many of the schools are still undergoing periods of substantial change. As we shared in the introduction to this book, the answer to the question of Christian school sustainability is not finding ways to continue doing exactly what we've done into the future; rather, sustaining our mission into the future will likely require finding very new and different ways to achieve that mission from what we have done in the past.

Although change is a constant in education, as organizational psychologist Harry Levinson says, "All change is loss, and loss must be mourned."[5] In *The Human Side of School Change*, Robert Evans points out that many change efforts in schools fail to take into account how people naturally react to change, which in turn sabotages efforts to reform or transform schools. As Evans writes,

> Significant change almost always means loss and causes a kind of bereavement . . . if, say, staff reductions result in our being transferred to a new school, leaving behind friends and status, or if after years of teaching advanced placement seniors we are suddenly forced to teach freshmen. A

major part of our world stops making sense; continuity is disrupted; our connections can no longer be counted on. Virtually nothing is more painful or more threatening to our basic security, our very ability to understand and cope with things. It is natural that we should vigorously avoid and resist such experiences.[6]

One of the potential benefits of taking disciplined risks is that it can generate more favorable conditions for individuals in schools—whether leaders, staff, or parents—to cope with the inevitable sense of loss that results from change. In other words, disciplined risk that is intentional, incremental, and iterative can help scaffold the experience of change for school constituencies, as compared with the more significant effects of radical or sudden change. And for schools that repeatedly take disciplined risks with demonstrated success over time, future changes may become easier as trust is built with the school community and relationships are strengthened through the change process. Thus, while not a silver bullet or magic wand for Christian school sustainability, taking disciplined risks can be a key for making necessary changes to schools' structural and financial models—and the priorities, programs, and people that are connected to them. Taking disciplined risk is good stewardship of the resources God provides and ultimately allows for productive change bounded by providential wisdom.

Disciplined risk that is intentional, incremental, and iterative can help scaffold the experience of change for school constituencies, as compared with the more significant effects of radical or sudden change.

PART THREE
PEOPLE AND COMMUNITY

CHAPTER SEVEN

PRIORITIZE PEOPLE

Our workplaces matter because they are human institutions filled with people whom God cares about. God wants all people to flourish and to be drawn into relationship with him. . . . Good and godly leadership contributes to human flourishing when it creates cultures and environments that are fair, just, and caring.

—Richard Stearns, *Lead Like It Matters to God*[1]

Research clearly demonstrates the importance of relationships and well-being in schools. Teachers are the most significant school-level influence on student learning,[2] and school administrators are the second most influential school-level factor.[3] For adults, the relationship between principals and teachers is key, with principals' leadership behaviors directly correlated with teachers' self-efficacy.[4] In the Christian school setting, ACSI's Flourishing Schools Research identified correlations between relational constructs and flourishing outcomes for both students and educators—such as Christlike teachers and mentorship for students, supportive leadership for teachers, and leadership interdependence for leaders and board members.[5]

As discussed in the introduction to this book, however, schools in all sectors are facing a human resource challenge. Across the field of education, teacher burnout, attrition, and shortages are prevalent.[6] School leader retention is also suffering in part because of the politically and culturally contentious climate in many school communities.[7] Christian schools are not immune to some of these challenges; for example, research on the Christian school sector documented widespread stress among both teachers and leaders even before the COVID-19 pandemic.[8] Research has also identified high turnover in school leadership and compensation rates that are significantly below that of other educational sectors.[9]

Arguably, long-term sustainability in the Christian school sector must address these human challenges. Even if somehow schools remain open into the future, they cannot truly be said to fulfill their missions if the adults and children within them are not thriving. According to Richard Stearns, "If God's kingdom is to expand and grow, every human institution must also be renewed by the values and principles of his kingdom."[10] Prioritizing people is aligned with the biblical foundation of Christian schools' missions. Gauging the degree to which schools put people first can be done by asking questions like, How does prioritizing people play out in school policy and leadership decisions? How do schools allocate resources in ways that prioritize the human endeavor that is central to Christian schools' missions? How does the use of finances reflect the value schools place on their people?

In this chapter, we examine three schools more closely to better understand how they are strategically investing in faculty and staff and liberating resources to prioritize people. While certainly no workplace is perfect, these schools recognize the importance of placing people before programs and buildings, both for long-term sustainability and fulfilling their God-given missions into the future.

Investing in Educators

While salaries often consume the majority of schools' budgets, leaders have a choice in how they view this expenditure—either as a necessary cost center to deliver their educational programs, or as a wise investment in the people who will help to fulfill their mission. Two schools in our study take the latter view, one by prioritizing competitive salaries as well as supporting educators' spiritual growth, and another that supports teachers in pursuing their passions within the classroom through substantial grants for innovation.

Valor Christian High School (Highlands Ranch, Colorado)

Regardless of the number of resources a school has, how they invest those resources demonstrates priorities. By most standards, Valor Christian High School is one of the best-resourced schools in our study. It is located in an affluent and growing suburb of Denver and, as the youngest school in our study, opened in 2007 with the backing of significant philanthropic investment. It would be a mistake, however, to discount Valor's emphasis on prioritizing people because of the size and scope of its resources. Rather, there are important lessons to be learned from the way leaders at Valor intentionally and systematically invest their resources first and foremost in their people, in alignment with their mission.

From the beginning, Valor prioritized teacher and staff salaries in their budgeting. To avoid losing teachers to surrounding public and private schools, they benchmark their salaries at the level of the highest-paying public schools in their area. The success of this approach in teacher retention is evident in the number of primary wage earners who are employed at Valor; former head of school Kurt

Unruh explained, "70 to 80 percent of our faculty and staff are primary wage earners in their family. We don't have a lot of people pulled away because of the job transfers of the primary wage earner."

The founding leaders' early decision to prioritize educator salaries gave birth to two specific funding strategies, both of which are relatively uncommon in Christian schools. First, the school has achieved a 105 percent hard income coverage ratio, which includes tuition and other operating income. This in contrast to the prevailing model in Christian schools, where hard income covers 80 percent of operating costs, and soft income streams (like fundraising) provide the remaining 20 percent—or, more commonly, educator salaries are set at significantly lower rates than local benchmarks, which effectively discounts the price of tuition at the cost of offering a competitive wage to teachers and staff. By having a hard income ratio at 105 percent, Valor can ensure that the real costs of competitive salaries are covered in the school's operating budget.

While this approach could easily price families even further out of the market for a Valor education, a second innovative strategy helps to mitigate this possibility. Instead of charging a tuition rate and offering commensurate financial aid that is subject to change on a yearly basis, Valor built a financial model whereby they offer each family a total four-year price for their student's Valor education, pro-rated equally across four years. This price includes school-side considerations like cost increases and strategic funding plans, as well as family-side considerations like financial aid needs. Of course, the amount of aid a family receives can be adjusted if there is a change in family circumstance, such as job loss or other significant life event that would affect the family's financial status. In general, however, this approach enables both the school *and* their families to engage in long-range financial planning, so that the funding priorities of the school can be met and families are assured that a Valor education will remain affordable across their student's high school experience.

In addition to these benefits to the school, educators, and families, Valor's prioritizing competitive salaries has enabled the school to be innovative and cutting-edge in its programs. Thanks in no small part to their compensation packages, Valor can hire talented individuals from industries outside of education who, most importantly, feel called to Valor's Christian mission. When asked about innovation at the school, leaders cited "atypical hiring" as one of the main drivers—meaning that teaching licensure is not required, as it would eliminate many talented candidates coming from industry who do not want to incur the costs of additional degrees. At the same time, Valor provides a strong mentorship program, which equips teachers who have a depth-of-life experience in other professions. This is evident in the hires that led to many of its education innovations, including the Valor Conservatory for the Arts with professional sound, dance, recording, and production studios; the Valor Institute for Applied STEM; the Valor Discovery service and intercultural learning program; and the Valor Sports Network. In all these areas, new faculty members have infused fresh perspectives and catalyzed innovation within the parameters of Valor's mission. One administrator at the school shared, "Given this entrepreneurial spirit, people have been allowed to flourish in their areas with far more creativity." At the same time, these hires still meet the school's rigorous requirements related to faith and Christian walk, as head of school Gary Fisher explained: "We go through a hiring grid process, and the key anchoring criteria is 'do they have an active faith in Jesus Christ?'" For talented people who are also devoted followers of Christ, Valor's approach to innovation through competence-driven autonomy is appealing.

Finally, like many Christian schools that have staff who oversee student life and discipleship, Valor also has a campus pastor on staff whose sole responsibility is the spiritual well-being of school leaders, faculty, and staff. Campus pastor Jim Kirchner highlighted the importance of supporting leaders and educators in their spiritual lives, explaining, "You can't give away what you don't have." According to Kirchner, key to his role is helping adults in the school through the inevitable tests and trials of both education and life, while maintaining and even drawing strength from the joy of the Lord (Nehemiah 8:10).

Through pastoral counseling, devotionals and Bible study, and other discipleship efforts, Kirchner aims to encourage and equip faculty to "live a compelling life that students would want to imitate." While not all Christian schools can support a full-time campus pastor for educators, all schools can intentionally strategize and systematize ways to encourage the spiritual well-being and growth of leaders, faculty, and staff—alongside their students.

Cincinnati Hills Christian Academy (Cincinnati, Ohio)

In the preceding chapter, we profiled the ways in which Cincinnati Hills Christian Academy (CHCA) takes disciplined risks through its innovative programming. Central to this programming, however, is the school's investment in its faculty as the drivers of innovation. As a leading innovator-teacher stated, "I think that a spirit of innovation comes out of the autonomy and the ability to bring whatever creativity you have to the classroom and the passions that teachers have around their subjects." One of the key means of supporting faculty is through the school's teacher innovation fund, which originated during the school's last capital campaign and resulted from 10 percent of funds raised—around $1.8 million—being allocated for the new fund.

CHCA has developed an application and committee review process by which teachers apply and are approved for individual grants, with the committee also providing teachers with guidance and help to develop proposals. Examples of grants awarded include a classroom redesign project, which paid for design experts to work with students in designing an optimal classroom space for learning. Another grant involved a schoolwide food symposium that brought celebrity chefs on campus and connected with the school's entrepreneurship and sustainability programming. A third involves a group of twenty-five faculty who constitute a "theological integration cohort" and, as part of their eighteen months of study together, traveled to Israel on an education tour; ultimately, this group will serve as trainers of other faculty on how to better integrate the school's theological "big ideas" into all curricula and areas of school life. Other grants are not as large, but one leader explained that they still have a sizeable impact: "There are some grant opportunities that were smaller and more localized within classrooms, but it's those kinds of things that are having deep impact in the long run because they speak directly to what students are doing to engage the content and have a lot of potential to ripple forward into good collaboration among teams and departments."

Not only has the teacher innovation fund influenced faculty and their classrooms individually, but it has also transformed the faculty culture at the school. One teacher shared, "I've used that fund two or three times to really get into some different ideas and plans that have really turned into some great things at the school because that funding was there." An instructional leader at the school shared that thanks to the innovation fund, many teachers' grants are now "a fully fledged program that's growing each day and you can really point to that innovation fund. And that initial grant that was given as a starting point of the whole thing." The excitement of teachers pursuing their passions through the grant has an impact even into the community; for both the classroom redesign and the food symposium projects, one leader reported that community partners who were involved "came away amazed, saying this is phenomenal. . . . They just had a lot of questions about how we were making this work."

While the monies from this fund are not directly paid to teachers, the fund still invests in educators in a meaningful way. Specifically, the fund recognizes teachers' desire and need for autonomy to direct and improve student learning on their own. As one instructional leader explained, the funds allow teachers to think and plan "outside the box of their regular school constructs, to do something that they think could benefit the school or benefit kids or do something different." This is significant, as ACSI's Flourishing Schools Research demonstrates the positive link between supportive leadership that empowers teachers to make decisions and flourishing outcomes in Christian schools.[11] In addition, this research found a strong correlation between the quality of student learning and teachers' job satisfaction: at Christian schools where student engagement in learning was significantly higher, teacher turnover was significantly lower.

The experience of CHCA's faculty may provide some insight into this correlation. As Stephen Carter, the school's director of entrepreneurship and sustainability, shared, "You have to have the funding to be innovative. But the other piece of this is that it is driven by the passions of the teacher." Another instructional leader explained of a fellow teacher who received a grant, "She's the one who had that idea. She's the one who was willing to take that risk. She was the one who was willing to ask her principal, 'Hey, how can I make this happen?' It's the people. And then we just encourage that as much as we possibly can." With the funding available to pursue their passions and take risks, teachers at CHCA are prioritized and energized to make changes in the classroom that improve their students' learning and engagement.

Liberating Resources

To understand what leaders value, we can look at how they allocate resources. In a world of scarce resources, spending money in one area necessarily means a school is not spending it in another area. The way our final school in this chapter allocates their funds is fully in line with their mission—and prioritizes people, by liberating resources that are often tied up elsewhere in Christian schools.

Chattanooga Christian Schools (Chattanooga, Tennessee)

Chattanooga Christian Schools (CCS) allocates resources in a very deliberate way that has allowed them to invest strategically in people. As already mentioned in a previous chapter, head of school Chad Dirkse does not have an office, so as to allow for more student learning space. This is just the tip of the iceberg when it comes to the ways that CCS puts their mission first when it comes to resource allocation. As the school's chief financial officer shared, "We want to spend our money the most wisely in accordance with our mission. . . .We just did an LED lighting study that saved us a ton of money. I'm always trying to look at things that we can be efficient with, so that we can always put that funding back to the student, back to the mission, back to what we do as a core."

Rather than expensive and more traditional buildings, the facilities on the main campus consist of entirely pre-engineered metal buildings. Dirkse refers to them as "grow spaces, not show places." The structures are useful for "building conduit through which teachers can engage students in relationships that produces purposeful work." The buildings are open-span buildings without interior load-bearing walls or support structures, so the school can reorganize spaces to respond to faculty and student needs at a low cost. The main campus is located in an up-and-coming, industrial area of the city, so Dirkse feels like the design aesthetic works for the school; he reported that donors and families appreciate the way CCS uses less expensive spaces, as well as design techniques like color blocking and abundant landscaping that enhance the overall feel of the campus (see photo insert). Combined with the school's strategy of opening microschools in partnership with area churches (versus building new campuses), this approach to facilities has made it possible for CCS to expand without taking on long-term debt—which in turn liberates even more resources to invest in people.

In addition to these savings on buildings and debt servicing, the school annually allocates 4 percent interest on their $8 million endowment to go entirely toward faculty compensation. Altogether, this enables the school to offer salaries that are equal to or higher than other private and public schools in the area. Even though they cannot match the retirement benefits offered in other educational sectors, the school's competitive salaries and a tuition benefit for children of faculty enables them to attract talented professionals who believe in the school's Christian mission. And by investing in a human resources director—a position that is relatively rare in Christian schools—the school can hire more effectively, maximizing their investment in individuals. The human resources director shared that she regularly asks two questions: "Who are we attracting? And how do we go through the vetting process to make sure we are hiring the right people?" This strategic, schoolwide approach to hiring is essential, because faculty salaries typically account for the majority of a school's budget.

Wherever they can, CCS leaders continually seek to free up financial resources to serve their mission more fully. By reducing expenses on facilities and making wise investments in human resources, CCS has been able to invest funding in hiring and retaining people who can serve students well. Even though the grounds may not have the "feel" of a more traditional private school, it is a vibrant, modern, and appealing campus. Most importantly, CCS can truly say that every dollar is directly invested in the school's mission to prepare students to serve and lead with distinction while representing Christ.

Facing the Human Resource Challenge

In efforts to transform their structural and financial models, Christian schools can easily gloss over the human side of schools. But in *The Courage to Teach*, Parker Palmer warns educational leaders, "In our rush to reform education, we have forgotten a simple truth: reform will never be achieved by renewing appropriations, restructuring schools, rewriting curricula, and revising texts if we continue to demean and dishearten the human resource called the teacher on whom so much depends."[12] In any plans for educational reform, Palmer asserts that teachers must be "better compensated, freed from bureaucratic harassment, given a role in academic governance, and provided with the best possible methods and materials"—but as importantly, schools must intentionally cultivate "the human heart that is the source of good teaching."[13] Addressing the human resource challenge facing education is essential if Christian schools are to be future-ready.

Addressing the human resource challenge facing education is essential if Christian schools are to be future-ready.

The schools highlighted in this chapter are doing just this, through their efforts to pay competitive wages, support faculty spiritually, enable faculty to pursue their passions, and free up resources for all of the above. Again, while no school is perfect, these Christian schools are working to address the human resource challenge in the education sector head-on. As mentioned in the beginning of this chapter, these challenges continue to grow; so too, then, must the importance of recruiting, retaining, and developing faculty and staff who thrive in a school community. When school models and budget priorities reflect this orientation, we are more likely to find joy-filled schools with educators pursuing truth, beauty, and wisdom alongside their students.

CHAPTER EIGHT

INVITE PARTNERS

If you want to go fast, go alone; if you want to go far, go together.

—African proverb

A two-story, student-painted mural of the proverb above hangs in one of the main stairwells at The City School's grade 6–12 Poplar Campus (see photo insert). Head of school Joel Gaines always makes this a stop on his school tour for visitors and explains that it is fundamental to the school's vision. Education is a complex, labor-intensive, and costly endeavor—one that schools will find difficult to go alone, no matter how well-resourced they are. More importantly for Christian schools, partnership is aligned with their biblically based missions. In

MindShift: Catalyzing Change in Christian Education, Daniel Pampuch and Darren Iselin point to the example of Jesus—"the Word became flesh and blood and moved into the neighborhood"—and assert that Christian schools must do likewise.[1]

There is compelling evidence that partnerships have a positive impact on schools from various sectors, including Christian schools. For example, partnership and trust between the school and community promotes sustained school growth as well as student academic achievement.[2] ACSI's Flourishing School Research found that the engagement of Christian school leaders with the surrounding community was positively linked with flourishing outcomes, including alumni reporting they are continuing to walk with God.[3] And consistent with this previous research, our quantitative survey for this study found having a close connection to the surrounding community to be significantly and robustly associated with optimism that the respondent's school would be open and more accessible in ten years (see appendix).

Despite these clear benefits, engagement with the surrounding community does not happen by accident. Rather, as Pampuch and Iselin explain, schools will need to exert intentional effort to combat the natural tendency of institutions toward "isolation, disengagement, or competitiveness."[4] In this chapter, we highlight how schools in our study have been proactive and strategic in forging partnerships with three key constituent groups in their surrounding community: with school families, with local churches and organizations, and with industry and businesses.

Partnering with Families

Not only does research demonstrate the benefits to students and the overall school community when strong parent partnerships exist with the school,[5] but also Christian schools usually see such partnerships as part of their mission. This is because most Christian schools view parents as the primary disciplers of their children as described in

Deuteronomy 6, and the Christian school's role as coming alongside and supporting parents in fulfilling their God-given responsibilities. For many Christian schools, however, genuine engagement with families is often aspirational.[6] One urban school in our study works hard to make strong partnerships a reality, and their example is more powerful as family engagement is often limited in urban settings because of school-level barriers that require intentional and innovative strategies if they are to be overcome.[7]

Hope Academy (Minneapolis, Minnesota)

As described in previous chapters, Hope Academy intentionally enrolls students from underserved populations. The student body is highly diverse, with 75 percent of students being ethnically non-white, and 37 percent coming from homes in which English is not the first language. Early on, leaders at Hope Academy recognized the need for family involvement in the school. The upper school principal shared, "We are viewing parents as partners and the most important educators in a child's life. We are trying to figure out how to partner with families who do not have the stability that they need."

Hope Academy employs multiple strategies to this end. First, the school hosts a number of family-involvement days when parents have the opportunity to visit their students' classes and experience lessons. Every October, families attend a ninety-minute session that equips them to support their students in key school initiatives like technology, cultural harmony, and trauma-informed parenting. School leaders also host Bible studies for parents and guardians. The school utilizes a family report card that lets parents and guardians know if they are fulfilling their part of the covenant they signed when their student was admitted. This type of intentionality has paid big dividends with parent-teacher conference participation rates of 96 percent. At the same time, Hope Academy leaders recognize that strong partnerships are not just about bringing families to campus. Rather, partnerships require meeting families where they are at. To this end, teachers conduct home visits for every student in October, which provides teachers with the chance to get to know families, learn about students' home life, and build relational bridges.

In addition, the Hope Academy team works to create a school culture that is welcoming to families and takes into consideration the unique needs of the community. For example, the school has also established a Cultural Harmony Team that meets monthly; a local black pastor works closely with the school and leads the team in better understanding the community they serve. This is important as the school is located in the Phillips neighborhood in Minneapolis, just fourteen blocks away from the site of the George Floyd murder and subsequent protests. Together the team has worked hard to understand and bring together a community that has been traumatized by racial violence for many years. The school has also invested heavily in professional learning for trauma-informed instruction. As a result of this professional learning and collaboration across grades, teachers reported they are well-versed in techniques to meet the needs of their students in ways that are atypical of most private school teachers.

Partnering with Local Churches and Organizations

In previous chapters we have highlighted schools for the way they have remained relevant to, and grown with, their local communities. For three of these schools, leveraging partnerships with local organizations and churches has been a critical strategy in their efforts, which in turn has also benefited their students through services and resources the schools could otherwise could not access or provide on their own.

The City School (Philadelphia, Pennsylvania)

We have previously discussed how the three campuses of The City School—located in the Spruce Hill, Fairmount, and Northern Liberties sections of Philadelphia—serve their neighbors through the leasing, renting, and donation of their facilities space to local groups and churches. This includes a neighborhood basketball program, a daycare facility, and three local churches that use their campuses for Sunday services. In addition to benefiting these groups that needed scarce and valuable facilities space in the city, the partnerships have also benefited The City School in tangible ways. For example, the church that meets in the school's Poplar Campus recently upgraded the technology in the school's gym with a large drop-down screen, lighting, and AV control system. In addition to the church services on Sunday, these resources are now used by the school for weekly chapels and other events.

This symbiotic relationship demonstrates the scriptural encouragement given by the apostle Paul to the body of Christ: "At the present time your plenty will supply what they need, so that in turn their plenty will supply what you need" (2 Corinthians 8:14 NIV). Moreover, the school and church can now allocate resources that they would have expended (on meeting space for the church, and on technology resources for the school) in other strategic places. By partnering and sharing together in kingdom-oriented ways, the school and the church are able to accomplish exponentially more—"to go far" together—in the words of the African proverb shared in the student-created mural on the campus.

Cincinnati Hills Christian Academy (Cincinnati, Ohio)

We have previously described the innovative and entrepreneurial nature of Cincinnati Hills Christian Academy (CHCA). Twenty miles from most of the school's campuses lies its Armleder campus, housed in the historic Crosley Square Building in downtown Cincinnati. Armleder thrives in part because of a few key strategic partnerships the school has made with community groups and resources. One critical partnership is with Talbert House, a nonprofit organization based in Cincinnati.[8] Talbert House was founded in 1965 and originally served homeless men, but today Talbert House provides a more comprehensive suite of services for women and children as well, with the mission of "empowering children, adults and families to live healthy, safe and productive lives" through addictions treatment, community care, court and corrections services, housing, and mental health services.

Through their partnership with CHCA's Armleder campus, Talbert House provides services for students with social-emotional needs. This partnership has enabled the school's students to access services that the school otherwise might not be able to provide, from a community partner who knows the downtown area and its needs best. Even though Talbert House is not a faith-based organization, the partnership has been successful and Armleder staff have had the opportunity to share the good work being done at the school to serve the community's students. As Armleder campus principal Cammie Montgomery explained, "It's important not to be an island. Use community resources, be creative about what's around you, and learn how you can be a service to these businesses and organizations as they partner with you."

Chattanooga Christian School (Chattanooga, Tennessee)

In addition to three churches that house microschools run by Chattanooga Christian School (CCS), the school also works with a number of non-Christian agencies and organizations both to serve their students and to be a good neighbor. As president Chad Dirkse shared, "Our partnerships model the relationships that we should be building across ideological and cultural lines." For example, the partnership between The Learning Center at the school with the Siskin Children's Institute has given the school access to expertise while crossing both ideological and cultural lines. Siskin Children's Institute was founded by Mose and Garrison Siskin, two Jewish businessmen and brothers from Chattanooga who were devoted to serving people with disabilities.[9] While a partnership between a Christian school and a Jewish medical center seem like an unlikely pairing, it has given CCS access to a level of medical expertise they could not have provided on their own. At the same time, the arrangement fits the school's partnership model because of its mutual benefits to the Siskin Children's Institute; Siskin has agreed to provide services at a lower cost because the partnership allows them to demonstrate their expertise in a K–12 setting. It has also given Siskin the trust and confidence to recommend the school to their own patients in their developmental preschool, in turn giving the school a new pipeline for enrollment.

Partnering with Industry and Businesses

Many specialized educational programs and courses—like those in STEM, the arts, and vocational-technical programs—require expensive equipment and materials. Generating the funding necessary to run these programs can prove challenging for many Christian schools. Partnerships with industry and local businesses can provide the opportunity to access these resources at a discounted price or even for free. And even for well-resourced schools or schools that are fortunate to have donors with related interests, such partnerships can be beneficial as they can both provide needed expertise for these programs and release the school to expend resources in other areas. Partnerships with industry and businesses can also enhance student learning and preparation not only by providing access to necessary equipment and resources but also by giving students real-life experience and connections with professionals in various fields.

We found several examples of these kinds of partnerships across the schools in our study, most of which we have already shared as ways that schools remain relevant, resource creatively, and take disciplined risks. These include the following:

- Cincinnati Hills Christian School's sustainability and entrepreneurship initiatives invite partnerships with local experts and businesses, who in turn share their expertise, donate equipment, and purchase produce and prepared foods from culinary students.

- The City School likewise partnered with Marc Vetri, a celebrity chef and award-winning restaurateur based in Philadelphia, to offer cooking classes to its middle schoolers and to serve as a site for Vetri's educational filming projects.

- Valor Christian High School set aside space in their Center for Culture and Influence through a small but centrally located art gallery, where local artists are invited to display their work alongside that of students; this in turn creates an entrée for artists to participate in the center's various other programs (see photo insert).

- Oaks Christian School formed a partnership with NASA Jet Propulsion Labs to work with their students in their IDEA (Innovation, Design, Engineering and Aeronautics) Lab.

- Chattanooga Christian School worked with local government agencies on a watershed project, which engaged students in constructing and beautifying a rain-collection field in the middle of the school's property.

- Lynden Christian School partners with local farms and construction sites to place students in jobs, while often reaping additional benefit from those relationships through used equipment that sites donate to the school's Career and Technical Education (CTE) programs.

Again, these partnerships are all win-win—schools and their students benefit from connections and resources from various industries and businesses, while the partnering companies and professionals receive something of value as well (such as promotional credit or access to students for internships). The schools in our study engaged in these partnerships vary significantly in terms of resources, size, and location, which suggests that partnering with industry and businesses can be a generative strategy for any Christian school.

From Practical to Missional

The schools' experiences shared in this chapter highlight the potential diversity of these partnerships. And while partnerships can be mutually beneficial, there is more to the partnerships in our study than just exchange of resources. Partnerships can be bridges, helping to release valuable expertise and resources in ways that enhance the education a school provides for its students. Partnerships can be clarifying, helping a school to go deeper into its core commitments. And partnerships can enrich communities, connecting both inside and outside the school through symbiotic relationships between a school, churches, and other organizations.

As CCS's Chad Dirkse explained, "There's the practical-application benefit of partnerships. And then there's the messaging—the storytelling part of partnerships that are really important." Partnerships can help Christian schools tell the larger story of how neighbors can know, serve, and love one another well. They can help Christian schools deepen their relationships with the families who enroll in the school and beyond, to the surrounding neighborhoods. As one leader shared in our study, a telling question for whether a school partners well is this: "If your school were to cease to exist, who would miss you?" The answer to this question—like partnerships themselves—is not only practical but also missional.

CHAPTER NINE

SHARE INNOVATION

Beneath the very best Mission True organizations are leaders who believe they have a calling beyond building their organizations. They see themselves as part of a much bigger team pursuing a much bigger mission.

—Peter Greer and Chris Horst, *Rooting for Rivals*[1]

It is our hope as authors that, like us, readers will be inspired by the stories of the schools in our study. These schools have worked hard toward achieving missional distinctiveness, relevancy to their communities, and inclusion of students with diverse backgrounds and abilities. They have resourced creatively, reimagined structures, and taken disciplined risks as they have implemented nontraditional models of school finance and operations. And in the process, they have prioritized their staff and invited partnerships with their communities. But for many of the schools we have profiled, their stories do not end there.

We have already seen how a single innovation at a school can create ripple effects throughout. For example, one successful merger might lead to additional mergers, or an innovative program might lead to the creation of other programs throughout a school. We call that an "innovation cascade," where momentum from the success of one innovation propels the school forward to develop new innovations. This cascade tended to strengthen the school's overall capacity to sustain a vibrant mission today and into the future. For some schools in our study, however, that cascade crossed over the boundaries of the school itself, as leaders connected and partnered with others and shared their innovations beyond their campus. For these schools, their focus expanded from internal sustainability to opportunities to strengthen others.

Once innovation spills beyond a single organization, it moves from an innovation cascade to what is known as "open innovation," where innovation can be shared quickly across networks of organizations. As Linus Dahlandar and Martin Wallin explain in an article for *Harvard Business Review*, "Open innovation has the potential to widen the space for value creation: It allows for many more ways to create value, be it through new partners with complementary skills or by unlocking hidden potential in long-lasting relationships."[2] Ultimately, open innovation among Christian schools is what can bring sector-level transformation and create a more dynamic ecosystem of future-ready Christian education.

Because of the promise of open innovation for Christian education writ large, this last chapter shares the ways that schools in our study have extended their innovations beyond their own campuses. We conclude with the proven benefits of sharing innovation across school networks and offer reflection questions for readers to consider how they can—in Peter Greer and Chris Horst's words in *Rooting for Rivals*—"see themselves as part of a much bigger team pursuing a much bigger mission."[3]

Extending Innovation Outward

By now, readers are familiar with the stories of the schools in our study. While their stories are far from over, this chapter shares the next steps in these schools' journeys as their innovations expand beyond their own campuses to reach and serve other Christian schools through collaboration, partnership, and networks.

Grand Rapids Christian Schools (Grand Rapids, Michigan)

In the early 2000s, Grand Rapids Christian Schools was in a state of crisis with significant debt and declining enrollment, particularly in its elementary schools located in neighborhoods located throughout the city. Since that time, Grand Rapids Christian Schools has regained a position of financial strength by becoming an innovator in creating new financial systems, merging schools to develop a multidimensional system, making a commitment to greater inclusion of students of all abilities, and being an incubator for curricular and school change. The school is now sharing their learning and expertise developed during this journey through a finance, business, and office-management arm that started by working with two local Christian schools that had neither the capacity nor the expertise needed to operate at a high level in those areas. This support quickly spread to a few more schools spanning the country, as Grand Rapids Christian Schools discovered its ability to support Christian schools' strategic efforts in both urban and rural communities. Even though the school may spin this business venture off into its own entity, it provides a great example of how schools can be open to serving needs within the broader Christian school community.

Oaks Christian School (Westlake Village, California)

As discussed in chapter 5, one of Oaks Christian School's key innovations is the development of their online program about ten years ago. Since then, Oaks Christian has begun to partner with Christian schools across the country to offer their online program. Partner schools utilize Oaks Christian Online courses in a variety of ways, including supplementing or enriching their course catalogs with classes they do not offer, as well as expanding their elementary grades into middle school without having to add buildings or significantly increase staff. As one Oaks Christian leader explained, developing the online program has enabled the school to not only serve the needs of their own students but provide "a support to Christian schools as well, who don't have an online program or have the resources of Oaks Christian to be able to put that together."

Christian School Association of Greater Harrisburg (Harrisburg, Pennsylvania)

Also in chapter 5, we profiled the Christian School Association of Greater Harrisburg (CSAGH), a school district in the Capitol District of Harrisburg that resulted from the joining together of two Christian schools on either side of the Susquehanna River. While the financial efficiencies weren't as significant as leaders had hoped in the short term, the creation of the district led to a greater professionalization of various areas like finance and development. This in turn contributed to greater stability in the district's financial position, with both schools now faring significantly better together than they were apart. As CSAGH's leaders have shared their story of kingdom-minded collaboration with other schools, the story has inspired the creation of another district in Pennsylvania, Alliance Christian School District, which is a merger of two schools about seventy miles east of Harrisburg.

Chattanooga Christian School (Chattanooga, Tennessee)

In earlier chapters we have described the innovative way that Chattanooga Christian School (CCS) partners with three area churches to host and run microschools throughout the city of Chattanooga.

In today's economic and cultural landscape, the strong partnerships the school has forged with these churches through collaboration and relationship-building serves as a model for Christian schools looking to expand their footprint, enrollment, and influence. In terms of sharing innovation within a broader context, this is the reverse story of many Christian schools—whereas in previous decades many Christian schools were founded by churches, CCS is now starting Christian schools within churches. Remarkably, the school has also partnered with other private schools in the Chattanooga area to secure guaranteed seats in their secondary schools for microschool graduates—thereby sharing with other private schools their innovational approach of creating educational access for children of all backgrounds in Chattanooga.

Hope Academy (Minneapolis, Minnesota)

Hope Academy has a dynamic mission as well as an innovative approach to funding and building usage. The school also emphasizes high-quality education with appropriately compensated and supported professionals. For these reasons, Hope became a destination for inspiration in the work of urban education for schools across the country. It soon became evident to leader Russ Gregg that there was an opportunity to partner with visionary leaders and urban start-ups to use Hope's model, not as a replication, but rather as inspiration and support for new founders. The resulting Spreading Hope Network is a cohort program that connects would-be school founders in a multiyear network that offers a marketplace and logistics analysis for community and school readiness, as well as the "Hope Plunge," which is a business and educational boot camp to prepare the leaders to launch their schools successfully. In the first three years of its founding, Spreading Hope incubated eleven schools in as many cities throughout the United States.

Cincinnati Hills Christian Academy (Cincinnati, Ohio)

As discussed in several chapters, the student-run coffee cart at Cincinnati Hills Christian Academy (CHCA) started close to ten years ago and has grown into what is now the Leaning Eagle Coffee Bar, a student-run business which grosses $50,000 per year. The coffee bar served as the inspiration for a business incubator that seeds resources for other entrepreneurial ventures, as well as the school's Entrepreneurship and Sustainability Program, which itself now features a teaching kitchen and greenhouse. The program's director, Stephen Carter, now shares what the school has learned through an entrepreneurship curriculum he has developed for other schools to use as part of online learning resources through the Seed Tree Group. In this way, CHCA's insights and practices around innovation, real-life learning, leadership development, business and management skills, and environmental sustainability are now available to other schools across the country.

Open Sky Education (Milwaukee, Wisconsin)

In several chapters, we've highlighted the work of Open Sky Education mostly through the work of the HOPE Christian Schools in Milwaukee. Open Sky operates six schools in Milwaukee, another HOPE Christian School in Racine, Wisconsin, and multiple charter schools in Arizona. At the same time Open Sky has been approached by start-ups, homeschool co-ops, and traditionally Lutheran parishes about revitalizing old school facilities for new Christian microschools. As these requests came pouring in, Open Sky started a committee of internal and external experts to determine the best steps for the development of these growing requests and seemingly endless opportunities. With a focus on their vision, but also seeing their strengths as a start-up and school operator, Open Sky added a school and business support arm called Soaring Education Services. This arm has already incubated and supported a few schools in their development and expects to work with over one hundred schools in the 2022–2023 school year.

Expanding Our Sense of Mission

From communities of practice[4] to professional learning communities[5] to networked improvement communities (NICs),[6] much has already been made in the literature about collaborative approaches to improvement in education. Collaboration among schools that work together in networks allows for broader experimentation, more rapid iteration, and greater possibility for scaling innovation. While we have mentioned that collaboration does not come easily for most schools, Christian schools are already well-positioned to lead the way because of their shared sense of mission, common bond through a shared faith, and an orientation toward improvement that is grounded in the confident humility[7] that comes from serving a Savior and purpose great than our own.

Since Peter Greer and Chris Horst wrote their inspirational book *Mission Drift* in 2014,[8] Christian organizations have rightly focused on ways to remain true to their mission for the long term. However, just four years later in their book *Rooting for Rivals*, the authors confessed that being "Mission True" takes more than protecting against drift:

> We've realized since writing *Mission Drift* that even if we get our own proverbial house in order, our broader mission will fail miserably if we stop there. We've come to believe that no matter how many guardrails we put in place or how many bylaws we draft to fend off drift, faith-based organizations cannot be Mission True unless they exist for a purpose beyond their own organizational borders.[9]

The implications for education are considerable, given that schools are often known more for competing—versus collaborating—with other schools. To shift from an organization-centric view to a sector-level view will be a challenge for schools, but it may be key to unlocking greater sustainability for both individual schools and Christian education as a whole.

Interestingly, research has demonstrated the importance of

kingdom-minded collaboration for Christian schools. ACSI's Flourishing Schools Research found that at schools where leaders prioritized engaging the community—which includes other schools—alumni were more than twice as likely to report that they were continuing to walk with God.[10] Similarly, in our quantitative survey analysis for the present study, we found that community engagement was associated with greater optimism that a respondent's school would remain open and be even more accessible in ten years (0.12–0.14 standard deviations; see appendix). Thus, while schools looking to strengthen spiritual outcomes wouldn't be wrong to start with their Bible curriculum and chapel programs, they also wouldn't be entirely right either. We may not fully understand why cooperation and partnership with those outside the school has a lasting positive impact on students, but we have a hunch: when school leaders look beyond themselves and their own campuses to engage and serve others, opportunities result for students to see more of the gospel "in action." As Greer and Horst explain, "We are not just building organizations . . . . We are participating in an eternal Kingdom. We are members of a community not marked by organizational boundaries but by the blood of our Savior . . . by self-sacrifice and love for those who could never repay Him."[11]

Questions for Reflection

Expanding our sense of mission to encompass other schools requires intentionality. To this end, we recommend gathering a group of leaders at your school (administrators as well as board members) and reflecting together on the following questions to gauge your school and team's readiness, identify your focus, and create a plan for action.

Questions to Gauge Our Readiness

1. As a leadership team and as a school, are we more collaborative or competitive with other schools?

2. If we already meet with other school leaders, how often do we do meaningful work together?

3. If we were to collaborate more closely or even partner with other schools, what do we have to lose as a school? What do we have to gain?

4. What barriers in our school's context, culture, or history keep us from being as collaborative or from partnering with other schools as we might wish?

5. Who needs to be involved in collaborating or partnering more closely with other schools, and how do we build capacity and release resources for these people to engage in this work (time, travel budget)?

Questions to Identify Our Focus

1. How future-ready is our school, and what are our top two or three "big questions" related to the sustainability of our school's mission into the future?

2. How does our school need to be more accessible or reach more students and families in our community?

3. What are the financial and structural innovations discussed in this book that are of greatest interest to us (mergers, online academies, microschools, school choice funding, Christian school districts, sharing backend functions, entrepreneurship, leasing, starting new schools, hybrid models, inclusion)?

4. What are the unique strengths of our school—things that are worth sharing with our community?

5. What innovations have we developed as a school that would be worth sharing with other schools and with the Christian school sector?

Questions to Plan for Action

1. What networks are we currently a part of that we can leverage for collaboration and partnership with other schools?

2. Where and how can we create new networks, where networks don't exist or our existing networks are insufficient?

3. What practices or routines do we need to put in to place, so we can share and exchange knowledge across these networks?

4. How can we look outside the Christian school sector for innovation—in other words, connecting our school with innovators in industry, business, and other fields?

5. When it comes to collaborating with other schools and partners, what are two or three concrete goals and related action steps we can set right now, for the coming six to twelve months?

As we shared at the beginning of this chapter, while the Christian schools in our study are better positioned for long-term, missional sustainability—thanks to their innovative school cultures, structures, and practices—there is more to their stories. As leaders have come to see themselves as part of something much bigger than just their own schools, they have invested time and resources in sharing their schools' innovations beyond their own campuses. It is this kind of networking that can lead to open innovation across the Christian school sector. As Christian educators see themselves—in the words of Greer and Horst—as part of a much bigger team with a much bigger mission, a more dynamic ecosystem of future-ready Christian education becomes truly possible.

EPILOGUE

We've used several metaphors to describe the journey that the schools in our study have taken toward greater long-term sustainability, missional growth, and increased reach within their communities. In the prologue to this book, we referenced Tim Elmore's language of schools and educators "marching off the map" of what's always been done in education, in order to prepare students more fully for today's world.[1] We also cited Tod Bolsinger's imagery of Lewis and Clark "canoeing the mountains," referring to the explorers abandoning the canoes that had been essential for their journey westward once they faced the Rockies.[2]

We want to close with two more metaphors that may be helpful in framing our schools' journeys and in expressing why we are hopeful for the future of Christian education. The first is that of "blocking and tackling," which originates in American football and refers to the need to be disciplined in sticking to the basics and succeeding at fundamental skills or tasks. Often when discussing issues around school sustainability, leaders will point to the importance of blocking and tackling versus taking innovative or untried approaches to a problem.

In writing this book, we are not suggesting that good practices related to financial management, policy governance, school leadership, and continuous improvement be tossed out the window—and the schools in our study didn't toss them out either. But the belief that blocking and tackling will always ensure success is entirely predicated on every playing field being level and standardized—for every single team and for every single game.

By way of contrast, Christian schools today are playing on fields that are unlevel, are not built to any uniform regulation or code, and are constantly changing. They also play in many different communities with unique resources, needs, challenges, and opportunities. Overall, the field of private schooling looks less like *Remember the Titans* these days and more like something out of an M.C. Escher painting or the dreamworld in the movie *Inception*. While the schools in our study never abandoned the essentials of playing the educational management game, they also realized that they needed new skills, team configurations, and game plans if they were to be successful on their educational playing fields. Their stories give us hope that other Christian schools, of all shapes, sizes, and locations, can do the same within their contexts.

The second metaphor is closely related to the first. A familiar aphorism (variously attributed to Abraham Maslow, Abraham Kaplan, Mark Twain, and a few others) goes like this: "If all you have is a hammer, then everything you see will look like a nail." In other words, if we only have one tool in our toolbox, we will frame every problem we encounter in terms of how we'll attack it with that tool. When a new challenge appears, instead of finding a new tool that is adapted to the specific challenge, we're more likely to grab the only tool we know how to use and begin pounding furiously away. This feels less risky at first because our favorite tool is comfortable and familiar to us, but working without the proper tool means there's actually a higher risk of failure—of botching the job and even causing collateral damage. This metaphor explains, at least in part, why so many of the speakers we have heard over the years are marketing, fundraising, development, and other "business model" experts who accurately describe the myriad sustainability challenges facing Christian schools, but only suggest better practices in those areas as the solution.

While marketing plans and annual campaigns are critically important, they cannot solve all the challenges facing Christian schools. Moreover, if done in isolation from a larger strategy, they only serve to reinforce the existing model of most Christian schools (tuition-driven and supplemented by philanthropy). We need new ideas for how we can respond to the adaptive challenges and changes facing our schools, education as a field, and our communities and world. The schools in our study moved beyond asking questions that "tinkered around the edges"—questions of how we can keep doing the same thing we are doing today but do it slightly better. They realized that adaptive-level challenges require adaptive-level solutions, which always seem radical and risky, but in reality are no more so than keeping the current course. The schools in our study give us hope because instead of relying on the single tool they had in their toolbox—doing things the "way we've always done them"—they added brand-new tools or retooled entirely.

Perhaps most importantly, the schools in our study expanded their repertoire of how to "do school" not just to respond to the increasingly complex problems they were facing but also to take advantage of the missional opportunities presented to them. This brings us back to our first chapter, where we borrowed James K.A. Smith's language of knowing what we love—because we are what we love, in that the things we love guide our priorities, decisions, and risks.[3] Fundamentally, the schools in our study all loved their Christ-centered missions more than the structures, models, and practices they used to achieve those missions. Because of that, they were willing to change—sometimes radically—how their schools look so those missions can be fulfilled into the future. And that makes us the most hopeful of all.

APPENDIX: QUANTITATIVE SURVEY DESIGN AND FINDINGS

In addition to Zoom focus groups, site visits, and interviews, we invited administrators, faculty and staff, and board members at the study's schools to complete a short survey in which they indicated how strongly they agree with sixteen items related to their perceptions of the school's sustainability, accessibility, and innovativeness on a four-point Likert scale (1 = Strongly disagree; 4 = Strongly agree). Survey items are summarized in table 1.

Sample

Overall, 553 respondents completed the survey representing the twelve schools in our sample, including 75 administrators, 318 teachers, 77 support staff, 14 board members, and 55 other members of the school community. Respondents indicating some other responsibility with the school included those working in admissions, athletics, counselling, and other responsibilities. The number of responses by school ranged from 1 to 107. The modal respondent was in his or her first year of employment at the school, with an average of 7.6 years of experience at the current school and a maximum of 31 years in the overall sample.

Survey Instrument

On average, respondents tended to agree with the statements presented as they pertain to their respective schools. Respondents agreed most strongly with item 11 ("Teacher relationships") and least strongly with item 13 ("Observations"). Administrators tended to be more likely to agree with the statements (the highest average response for 9 of the 16 items), and board members were least likely to agree (the lowest average response for 12 of the 16 items), though this general observation varies from item to item.

As we did not intend to uncover latent factors in our survey design, we identified covariate groupings using principal components analysis. This analysis yielded four components with eigenvalues exceeding one (see figure 1). Together, these four components cumulatively explain nearly 60 percent of the variation. Because the survey was not designed to have theoretically discrete components, we used a promax oblique rotation, allowing components to be correlated with each other, though orthogonal rotations yield similar component groupings. We label the four components "Commitment to access," "Openness to change," "Quality of relationships," and "Optimism about the school's future" (see tables 2–5).

Empirical Strategy

To descriptively test relationships between components and optimism about the school's future, we regress each item measuring optimism about the school's future using the following model:

$$y_i = \beta_0 + \kappa_i' \beta + X_i' \beta + \epsilon_i$$

where y_i represents a standardized measure of respondent i's optimism that the school will be open or more accessible in 10 years, κ_i' is a row vector of component variables for "Commitment to access," "Openness to change," or "Quality of relationships," standardized with a mean of 0 and a standard deviation of 1, and ϵ_i is an idiosyncratic error term.

In our fully specified model, we include X_i', a vector of respondent i's demographic characteristics including role and experience, to test for the robustness of the relationships between components and optimism to the inclusion or exclusion of these covariates. As this analysis is descriptive and exploratory, we consider estimates with a p-value less than 0.01 (α = 0.99) in order to minimize the risk of Type I errors.

Results

Commitment to Access and Optimism

"Support underserved students" is positively and significantly associated with greater optimism that the school will be both open and more accessible in ten years. "Welcoming" significantly associated with "more accessible" with demographic controls, but not in models with no covariates. "Innovative access" was significantly associated with "more accessible" in models with no covariates, but not in models with respondent controls. We estimate that agreeing more strongly that one's school supports underserved students by one standard deviation was associated with a 0.25 standard deviations greater optimism that the school would be open in ten years, and with 0.18–0.19 standard deviations greater optimism that the school would be more accessible in ten years.

Openness to Change and Optimism

"Change" and "Community" are positively and significantly associated with greater optimism that the school will be both open and more accessible in ten years. We estimate that agreeing more strongly that one's school welcomes change by one standard deviation was associated with 0.15–0.16 standard deviations greater optimism that the school would be open in ten years and 0.25–0.26 standard deviations greater optimism that the school would be more accessible in ten years. We also estimate that agreeing more strongly that a school seeks feedback from the community by one standard deviation was associated with

0.13–0.14 standard deviations greater optimism that the school would be open in ten years and 0.12 standard deviations greater optimism that the school would be more accessible in ten years.

Quality of Relationships and Optimism

Generally, the relationships component is positively and significantly associated with greater optimism that the school will be both open and more accessible in ten years. Good working relationships with administrators associated with greater optimism that the school will be both open and more accessible. Good working relationships with teachers associated with greater optimism that the school will be open (robust across specifications) and associated with greater optimism that the school will be more accessible, but only when controlling for demographic characteristics. We estimate that agreeing more strongly regarding the quality of teacher relationships by one standard deviation was associated with 0.16–0.19 standard deviations greater optimism that the school would be open in ten years. We also estimate that agreeing more strongly regarding the quality of administrator relationships by one standard deviation was associated with 0.22–0.24 standard deviations greater optimism that the school would be open in ten years and 0.20–0.22 standard deviations greater optimism that the school would be more accessible in ten years.

Discussion

Robust across model specifications, four items—effectively supporting underserved students, welcoming change, having a close connection with the surrounding community, and having good working relationships with administrators—are positively and significantly associated with optimism that the school will be both open and more accessible in ten years.

With respect to survey instrumentation, we note one divergence from theoretical expectations. Principal components analysis yielded that a school's relationship with its surrounding community was closely related to its openness to change. We expected a school's relationship with the surrounding community to be more closely related to other items probing a respondent's relationships. This grouping suggests that the "openness to change" component grouping may be capturing a school's willingness to "change with their community."

Descriptively, different school community members express varying levels of willingness to agree with the statements presented. In general, administrators were the most likely to agree and should be cautioned to be aware that other constituents may not be as likely to agree. Board members tended to be the least likely to agree with the statements presented, with several notable exceptions: board members seem to be most cognizant of community relations, most likely to agree that the school "welcomes underserved students," and that the school "has a close connection to the surrounding community."

It is important to note that survey respondents believe that commitment to access is not "merely" about access, but about the sustainability of the school's mission into the future. Respondents who perceived their school to be committed to access were more optimistic that the school would be both open and more accessible in the future. These patterns of responses reveal that respondents believe that a school's ability to make itself more accessible to a more inclusive body of students is connected with its long-term sustainability. In our qualitative research, we find evidence of the importance of both increasing access and "changing with the community." Many school leaders expressed the importance of adopting strategies to adapt to demographic changes in the local community, taking steps to represent a more ethnically and culturally diverse student population today. Improving accessibility also includes making the school inclusive of a broader swath of the general population, including learners of diverse abilities.

Relationships, both with teachers and administrators, are key to respondents' optimism of the school's sustainability. "Good working relationships with teachers" was positively and significantly associated with optimism that the school will be open, though not necessarily more accessible in ten years ($p < 0.05$ without controls and $p < 0.01$ with controls). "Good working relationships with administrators" was positively and significantly associated with optimism that the school will be open and more accessible across all model specifications. We do not, however, find that a shared vision between teachers and administrators was strongly correlated with optimism about the school's future. In our qualitative research, we consistently document evidence across all schools studied that affirms the importance of relationships.

Of course, it is important to note some limitations of our survey methodology. Our survey depended on a sample of convenience, and not a representative sample of administrators, teachers, staff, board members, and other school constituents. Nor is our sample of schools representative of Christian schools writ large. Finally, our survey items only capture perceptions of sustainability, innovation, and access.

Nonetheless, the survey findings have some value and informed our qualitative analysis school-level data. Estimates are fairly robust to the inclusion or exclusion of control covariates, with little change to point estimates, suggesting minimal mediatorial role. Regardless of the respondents' role with the school or the number of years of experience with the current school, respondents report similar relationships between components and optimism. We intentionally set a high confidence level for our findings ($\alpha = 0.99$), minimizing the risk of Type I errors. It may be that many more factors are strongly correlated with respondents' optimism of their school's sustainability and accessibility.

Tables and Figures

Table 1. Survey Items

#	Item	Abbreviation
1	Expanding access to underserved students is important to our school.	Expanding access
2	There is a shared vision between teachers and administrators, for increased access for underserved students.	Shared vision
3	Our school's approach to increased access for underserved students is innovative.	Innovative access
4	Our school welcomes underserved students.	Welcoming
5	Administrators collaborate with teachers to determine innovative approaches to instruction for underserved students.	Collaboration
6	Our school effectively supports underserved students.	Support underserved students
7	There are adequate resources to support our school's goals for increasing access for students.	Adequate resources
8	Risk-taking informed by reflection is encouraged.	Risk-taking
9	Our school regularly solicits feedback for improvement from the school community.	Feedback
10	Our school welcomes change.	Change
11	I have good working relationships with teachers.	Teacher relationships
12	I have good working relationships with administrators.	Administrator relationships
13	There is adequate time for teachers to observe each other teach.	Observations
14	Our school has a close connection to the surrounding community.	Community connection
15	Our school will be open to students ten years from now.	Open
16	Our school will be accessible to more students in ten years than it is today.	More accessible

Table 2. Commitment to Access*

#	Item	Abbrev.	Admin	Teacher	Staff	Board	Other
1	Expanding access to underserved students is important to our school.	Expanding access	**3.5**	3.3	3.3	*3.2*	3.4
2	There is a shared vision between teachers and administrators for increased access for underserved students.	Shared vision	**3.1**	3.1	3.1	*2.8*	3.0
3	Our school's approach to increased access for underserved students is innovative.	Innovative access	**2.9**	2.8	2.7	*2.6*	2.8
4	Our school welcomes underserved students.	Welcoming	3.4	*3.3*	3.3	**3.4**	3.4
6	Our school effectively supports underserved students.	Supports underserved students	2.9	2.9	2.9	*2.6*	**2.9**
	N min		75	311	76	13	54
	N max		75	318	77	14	55

*Highest average score for each item bolded. Lowest average score for each item italicized.

Table 3. Openness to Change*

#	Item	Abbrev.	Admin	Teacher	Staff	Board	Other
8	Risk-taking informed by reflection is encouraged.	Risk-taking	**3.1**	2.9	3.0	*2.7*	2.9
9	Our school regularly solicits feedback for improvement from the school community.	Feedback	**3.2**	3.0	*2.8*	2.9	3.1
10	Our school welcomes change.	Change	2.9	3.1	2.9	*2.7*	**3.1**
13	There is adequate time for teachers to observe each other teach.	Observations	2.3	2.3	2.4	*2.3*	**2.5**
14	Our school has a close connection to the surrounding community.	Community	3.0	2.9	2.9	**3.3**	3.0
	N min		70	313	74	12	50
	N max		75	316	77	14	55

*Highest average score for each item bolded. Lowest average score for each item italicized.

Table 4. Quality of Relationships*

#	Item	Abbrev.	Admin	Teacher	Staff	Board	Other
11	I have good working relationships with teachers.	Teacher relationships	3.5	**3.7**	3.5	*3.2*	3.6
12	I have good working relationships with administrators.	Administrator relationships	**3.6**	3.5	3.3	*3.1*	3.5
	N min			74	315	77	13	54
	N max			75	317	77	14	54

*Highest average score for each item bolded. Lowest average score for each item italicized.

Table 5. Optimism about the School's Future*

#	Item	Abbrev.	Admin	Teacher	Staff	Board	Other
15	Our school will be open to students ten years from now.	Open	**3.7**	*3.5*	3.5	3.5	3.6
16	Our school will be accessible to more students in ten years than it is today.	More accessible	**3.5**	3.2	3.2	*2.9*	3.3
	N min			74	313	76	14	52
	N max			75	314	76	14	53

*Highest average score for each item bolded. Lowest average score for each item italicized.

Table 6. Commitment to Access and Optimism

	Open		More Accessible	
	(1)	(2)	(3)	(4)
Expanding access	0.07	0.06	0.06	0.06
	(0.06)	(0.06)	(0.06)	(0.06)
	0.217	0.302	0.273	0.320
Shared vision	-0.08	-0.07	0.03	0.03
	(0.06)	(0.06)	(0.05)	(0.05)
	0.173	0.214	0.598	0.592
Innovative access	0.08	0.08	0.14	0.12
	(0.06)	(0.06)	(0.05)	(0.05)
	0.169	0.155	0.009*	0.021
Welcoming	0.05	0.04	0.13	0.14
	(0.05)	(0.05)	(0.05)	(0.05)
	0.350	0.421	0.010	0.008*
Support underserved	0.25	0.25	0.18	0.19
students	(0.05)	(0.05)	(0.05)	(0.05)
	0.000*	0.000*	0.000*	0.000*
Controls				
Role		X		X
Experience		X		X
n	523	523	526	526

Notes. Standard errors reported in parentheses. p-values reported below standard errors. $* p < 0.01$.

Table 7. Openness to Change and Optimism

	Open		More Accessible	
	(1)	(2)	(3)	(4)
Risk-taking	0.05	0.03	0.12	0.11
	(0.05)	(0.05)	(0.05)	(0.05)
	0.372	0.522	0.012	0.023
Feedback	0.13	0.13	0.03	0.01
	(0.05)	(0.05)	(0.05)	(0.05)
	0.011	0.011	0.525	0.811
Change	0.15	0.16	0.25	0.26
	(0.05)	(0.05)	(0.05)	(0.05)
	0.004*	0.002*	0.000*	0.000*
Observations	0.05	0.05	0.06	0.06
	(0.05)	(0.05)	(0.05)	(0.05)
	0.332	0.281	0.215	0.196
Community	0.14	0.13	0.12	0.12
	(0.05)	(0.05)	(0.04)	(0.05)
	0.003*	0.005*	0.006*	0.006*
Controls				
Role		X		X
Experience		X		X
n	510	509	511	510

Notes. Standard errors reported in parentheses. p-values reported below standard errors. $* \, p < 0.01$.

Table 8. Quality of Relationships and Optimism

	Open		More accessible	
	(1)	(2)	(3)	(4)
Teacher relationships	0.16	0.19	0.12	0.15
	(0.05)	(0.05)	(0.05)	(0.05)
	0.002*	0.000*	0.024	0.005*
Administrator	0.24	0.22	0.22	0.20
relationships	(0.05)	(0.05)	(0.05)	(0.05)
	0.000*	0.000*	0.000*	0.000*
Controls				
Role		X		X
Experience		X		X
n	530	529	531	530

Notes. Standard errors reported in parentheses. *p*-values reported below standard errors. * $p < 0.01$.

Figure 2. Scree Plot of Eigenvalues

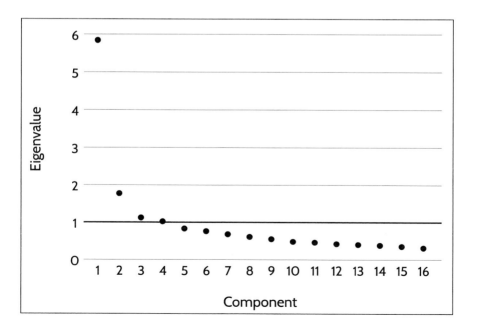

NOTES

Preface

1. T. Bolsinger, *Canoeing the Mountains: Christian Leadership in Uncharted Territory* (Downers Grove, IL: InterVarsity Press, 2015), 27.
2. Bolsinger, *Canoeing the Mountains*, 19.
3. T. Elmore, and A. McPeak, *Marching Off the Map: Inspire Students to Navigate a Brand New World* (Atlanta: Poet Gardener Publishing, 2017), 21.
4. Elmore and McPeak, *Marching Off the Map*, 22.
5. Elmore and McPeak, *Marching Off the Map*, 21.
6. L.E. Swaner, D. Beerens, and E. Ellefsen, eds., *MindShift: Catalyzing Change in Christian Education* (Colorado Springs, CO: Association of Christian Schools International, 2019).
7. D. Beerens and E. Ellefsen, "Epilogue: To Love Is to Risk," in Swaner, Beerens, and Ellefsen, *MindShift*, 125.

Introduction

1. In Christ Communications, "Landmark Summit Survey Reveals Encouraging Signs for Christian School Movement as Leaders Commit to Innovate," press release, March 22, 2019, http://inchristcommunications.com/portfolio/landmark-summit-survey-reveals-encouraging-signs-for-christian-school-movement-as-leaders-commit-to-innovate/.

2. Barna Group and the Association of Christian Schools International, *Multiple Choice: How Parents Sort Education Options in a Changing Market* (Colorado Springs: ACSI; Ventura, CA: Barna Group, 2017).

3. Pew Research Center, "America's Changing Religious Landscape," May 12, 2015, https://www.pewforum.org/2015/05/12/americas-changing-religious-landscape/.

4. S. Barrows et al., "Do Charters Pose a Threat to Private Schools? Evidence from Nationally Representative Surveys of U.S. Parents," *Journal of School Choice* 13, no. 1 (2019): 10–32.

5. ACSI, "2018–2019 Tuition & Salary Survey Member Report," Association of Christian Schools International, 2019.

6. ACSI, "2018–2019 Tuition & Salary Survey Member Report." As cited, and unless otherwise noted, data on the Christian-school sector is taken from the ACSI's data sets. ACSI is the largest Protestant school organization in North America, with close to 2,500 members across the United States and Canada; therefore data from ACSI schools can be viewed as broadly representative of the sector.

7. EdChoice, "The ABCs of School Choice: The Comprehensive Guide to Every Private School Choice Program in America," 2021, https://www.edchoice.org/wp-content/uploads/2021/03/2021-ABCs-of-School-Choice-WEB-2-24.pdf.

8. L.E. Swaner and M.H. Lee, *Christian Schools and COVID-19: 2020–2021 School Year Profile* (Colorado Springs: Association of Christian Schools International, 2020).

9. ACSI, "2018–2019 Tuition & Salary Survey Member Report."

10. NCES, "Racial/Ethnic Enrollment in Public Schools," *The Condition of Education in 2020: Elementary and Secondary Enrollment*, 2020, https://nces.ed.gov/programs/coe/pdf/coe_cge.pdf.

11. ACSI, "2018–2019 Tuition & Salary Survey Member Report."

12. R.A. Noël, "Race, Economics, and Social Status," *U.S. Bureau of Labor Statistics; Spotlight on Statistics*, 2018, https://www.bls.gov/spotlight/2018/race-economics-and-social-status/pdf/race-economics-and-social-status.pdf.

13. K.M. Chapman Jr., "Diversity in the Christian School: Retention Is About the Environment You Create," Center for the Advancement of Christian Education (blog), September 10, 2020, https://cace.org/diversity-in-the-christian-school-retention-is-about-the-environment-you-create/.

14. L.E. Swaner and J. Ferguson, "Christian School Leadership: 2019 ACSI Profile," *ACSI blog*, February 4, 2020, https://blog.acsi.org/christian-school-leadership-2019-acsi-profile; C.C. Miller, "Does Teacher Diversity Matter in Student Learning?," *The Upshot* (blog), *New York Times*, September 10, 2018, https://www.nytimes.com/2018/09/10/upshot/teacher-diversity-effect-students-learning.html.

15. J.A. Murray, "By the Numbers: A Clarion Call for Diversity, Equity, and Inclusion," *ACSI blog*, July 7, 2020, https://blog.acsi.org/call-for-diversity-equity-and-inclusion.

16. ACSI, "2018–2019 Tuition & Salary Survey Member Report."

17. NCES, "Students with Disabilities," *The Condition of Education in 2021: Elementary and Secondary Enrollment*, 2021, https://nces.ed.gov/programs/coe/pdf/2021/cgg_508c.pdf.

18. ACSI, "2018–2019 Tuition & Salary Survey Member Report."

19. E.L. Dombrowski and M.H. Lee, "Reimagining Finance and Sustainability: From Limits to Possibilities," in *ACSI Leading Insights: Special Education and Inclusion*, ed. L.E. Swaner (Colorado Springs: Association of Christian Schools International, 2021), 85–95.

20. Swaner and Lee, *Christian Schools and COVID-19: 2020–2021 School Year Profile*.

21. L.E. Swaner, *Professional Development for Christian School Educators and Leaders: Frameworks and Best Practices* (Colorado Springs: Association of Christian Schools International, 2016).

22. J.L. van der Walt and G. Zecha, "Philosophical-Pedagogical Criteria for Assessing the Effectiveness of a Christian School," *Journal of Research on Christian Education* 13, no. 2 (2004): 167.

23. D. Reynolds et al., *Educational Effectiveness Research (EER): A State of the Art Review* (Cyprus: International Congress for School Effectiveness and Improvement, 2011); D. Muijs et al., "Improving Schools in Socioeconomically Disadvantaged Areas: A Review of Research Evidence," *School Effectiveness and School Improvement* 15, no. 2 (2004): 149–75; A. Harris et al., "Improving Schools in Challenging Contexts: Exploring the Possible," *School Effectiveness and School Improvement* 17, no. 4 (2006): 409–24.

24. A. Crouch, K. Keilhacker, and D. Blanchard, "Leading Beyond the Blizzard: Why Every Organization Is Now a Startup," *Praxis Journal*, March 20, 2020, https://journal.praxislabs.org/leading-beyond-the-blizzard-why-every-organization-is-now-a-startup-b7f32fb278ff.

25. ACSI, "2018–2019 Tuition & Salary Survey Member Report"; ACSI, "2020–2021 Tuition & Salary Survey Member Report," Association of Christian Schools International, 2021.

26. L.E. Swaner and C. Marshall Powell, *Christian Schools and COVID-19: Responding Nimbly, Facing the Future* (Colorado Springs: Association of Christian Schools International, 2020).

27. Swaner and Lee, *Christian Schools and COVID-19: 2020–2021 School Year Profile*.

28. C. Waite and T. Arnett, *Will Schools Change Forever?* (San Francisco: Christensen Institute, 2020), 3.

29. L.E. Swaner, C. Dodds, and M.H. Lee, *Leadership for Flourishing Schools: From Research to Practice* (Colorado Springs: Association of Christian Schools International, 2021).

30. Swaner and Ferguson, "Christian School Leadership"; M.H. Lee, A. Cheng, and K. Wiens, *2020 Principal Survey* (Kennesaw: Council on Educational Standards & Accountability).

31. Swaner and Lee, *Christian Schools and COVID-19: 2020–2021 School Year Profile*.

32. M. Will, "Teachers Are Not OK, Even Though We Need Them to Be," *EdWeek*, September 14, 2021, https://www.edweek.org/teaching-learning/teachers-are-not-ok -even-though-we-need-them-to-be/2021/09; T. Walker, "Educators Ready for Fall, but a Teacher Shortage Looms," *National Education Association (NEA) News*, June 17, 2021, https://www.nea.org/advocating-for-change/new-from-nea/educators-ready-fall-teacher-shortage-looms.

33. NASSP, "NASSP Survey Signals a Looming Mass Exodus of Principals from Schools," *National Association of Secondary School Principals Bulletin*, December 8, 2021, https://www.nassp.org/news/nassp-survey-signals-a-looming-mass-exodus-of-principals-from-schools/.

34. M.H. Lee, R. Djita, and Cheng, "Sabbath Practices and Wellness in Christian Schools," *ACSI Research in Brief* 2, no. 2 (2021): 6–10; R.M. Miller and G. Hill, "Educator Well-Being: What About Leaders and Teachers?," in *ACSI Leading Insights: Mental Health and Well-Being*, ed. L.E. Swaner (Colorado Springs: Association of Christian Schools International).

35. Swaner, *Professional Development*.

36. L.E. Swaner, D. Beerens, and E. Ellefsen, eds., *MindShift: Catalyzing Change in Christian Education* (Colorado Springs: Association of Christian Schools International, 2019).

37. J. Murphy, *Leading School Improvement: A Framework for Action* (West Palm Beach, FL: Learning Sciences International, 2016), 37.

38. L.A. Hill et al., *Collective Genius: The Art and Practice of Leading Innovation* (Boston: Harvard Business Review Press, 2014), 3.

39. T. Cooling and E.H. Green, "Competing Imaginations for Teaching and Learning: The Findings of Research into a Christian Approach to Teaching and Learning Called What If Learning," *International Journal of Christianity & Education* 19, no. 2 (2015): 96–107.

40. A. Castellon and A. Jule, "Pursuing Excellence in Christian Education: Case Studies," Cardus, 2020, https://www.cardus.ca/research/education/reports/pursuing-excellence-in-christian-education-school-leadership/.

41. R. Yin, *Case Study Research: Design and Method*, 5th ed. (Los Angeles: Sage, 2014).

42. J.M. Stavros, L.N. Godwin, and D.L. Cooperrider, "Appreciative Inquiry: Organizational Development and the Strengths Revolution," in *Practicing Organization Development: Leading Transformation and Change*, ed. W.J. Rothwell, J.M. Stavros, and R.L. Sullivan, 4th ed. (San Francisco: Pfeiffer, 2016), 97.

43. Independent School Management, "ISM Theory for Consortium Members," 2012.

44. H.J. Rubin and I.S. Rubin, *Qualitative Interviewing: The Art of Hearing Data* (Los Angeles: Sage, 2005).

45. M. Patton, *Qualitative Research and Evaluation Methods* (Los Angeles: SAGE, 2002).

Chapter One

1. J.K.A. Smith, *You Are What You Love: The Spiritual Power of Habit* (Grand Rapids: Brazos, 2016), 1 (emphases original).
2. P. Greer, C. Horst, and A. Haggard, *Mission Drift: The Unspoken Crisis Facing Leaders, Charities, and Churches* (Minneapolis: Bethany House, 2014).
3. Greer, Horst, and Haggard, *Mission Drift*, 75
4. D. Beerens and E. Ellefsen, "Epilogue: To Love Is to Risk," in *MindShift: Catalyzing Change in Christian Education*, ed. L.E. Swaner, D. Beerens, and E. Ellefsen (Colorado Springs: Association of Christian Schools International, 2019), 125.
5. Greer, Horst, and Haggard, *Mission Drift*, 71–72 (emphases original).
6. Greer, Horst, and Haggard, *Mission Drift*, 72.
7. Smith, *You Are What You Love*, 27.

Chapter Two

1. C.W. Brooks, *Urban Apologetics: Why the Gospel Is Good News for the City* (Grand Rapids: Kregel, 2014), 29.

Chapter Three

1. I.L. Ince Jr., *The Beautiful Community: Unity, Diversity, and the Church at Its Best* (Downers Grove, IL: InterVarsity, 2020), 42.
2. ACSI, "2018–2019 Tuition & Salary Survey Member Report," Association of Christian Schools International, 2019.
3. EdChoice, "The ABCs of School Choice: The Comprehensive Guide to Every Private School Choice Program in America," 2021, https://www.edchoice.org/wp-content/uploads/2021/03/2021-ABCs-of-School-Choice-WEB-2-24.pdf.
4. NCES, "Racial/Ethnic Enrollment in Public Schools," *The Condition of Education in 2020: Elementary and Secondary Enrollment*, 2020, https://nces.ed.gov/programs/coe/pdf/coe_cge.pdf.
5. ACSI, "2018–2019 Tuition & Salary Survey Member Report."
6. R.A. Noël, "Race, Economics, and Social Status," *U.S. Bureau of Labor Statistics*; Spotlight on Statistics, 2018, https://www.bls.gov/spotlight/2018/race-economics-and-social-status/pdf/race-economics-and-social-status.pdf.
7. K.M. Chapman Jr., "Diversity in the Christian School: Retention Is About the Environment You Create," *Center for the Advancement of Christian Education* (blog), September 10, 2020, https://cace.org/diversity-in-the-christian-school-retention-is-about-the-environment-you-create/.
8. L.E. Swaner and J. Ferguson, "Christian School Leadership: 2019 ACSI Profile," *ACSI blog*, February 4, 2020, https://blog.acsi.org/christian-school-leadership-2019-acsi-profile; C.C. Miller, "Does Teacher Diversity Matter in Student Learning?," *The Upshot* (blog), New York Times, September 10, 2018, https://www.nytimes.com/2018/09/10/upshot/teacher-diversity-effect-students-learning.html.

9. Murray, "By the Numbers."

10. L.E. Swaner, C.A. Marshall, and S.A. Tesar, *Flourishing Schools: Research on Christian School Culture and Community* (Colorado Springs: Association of Christian Schools International, 2019).

11. K.E. Strater, "A Review of the Research on Inclusive Christian Education," In *ACSI Leading Insights: Special Education and Inclusion*, ed. L.E. Swaner (Colorado Springs: Association of Christian Schools International, 2021), 38–49.

12. M.T. Moore et al., *Patterns in Special Education Service Delivery and Cost* (Washington, DC: Decision Resources, 1988); J.G. Chambers, T. Parrish, and J.J. Harr, *What Are We Spending on Procedural Safeguards in Special Education, 1999–2000?* (Palo Alto, CA: Special Education Expenditure Project, Center for Special Education Finance, American Institutes for Research, 2002); J. J. Harr-Robins, and J.G. Chambers, "Special Education," in *Handbook of Research in Education Finance and Policy*, 2nd edition, ed. H.F. Ladd, and M.E. Goertz (New York: Routledge, 2015), 567–584.

13. M. Claypool and J. McLaughlin, "Why Improving America's Understanding of Special Needs Will Lead to More Educational Choice," EdChoice, August 2, 2017, https://www.edchoice.org/engage/improving-americas-understanding-special-needs-will-lead-educational-choice/.

14. J.P. Greene and S. Buck, "The Case for Special Education Vouchers," *Education Next* 10, no. 2 (2010): https://www.educationnext.org/the-case-for-special-education-vouchers/; J.P. Greene and G. Forster, "Vouchers for Special Education Students: An Evaluation of Florida's McKay Scholarship Program," Center for Civic Innovation at the Manhattan Institute, Civic Report 38, 2003, https://media4.manhattan-institute.org/pdf/cr_38.pdf; V.R. Weidner and C.D. Herrington, "Are Parents Informed Consumers: Evidence from the Florida McKay Scholarship Program," *Peabody Journal of Education* 81, no. 1 (2006): 27–56; A. Cheng and E.E. Coady, "An Evaluation of Florida's McKay and Gardiner Scholarship Programs" (paper presented at the Ninth Annual International School Choice and Reform Conference [virtual], 2021).

15. L.E. Swaner and M.H. Lee, *Christian Schools and COVID-19: 2020–2021 School Year Profile* (Colorado Springs: Association of Christian Schools International, 2020).

16. Swaner, Marshall, and Tesar, *Flourishing Schools*.

17. ACSI Research, "Insights from Flourishing Schools Research," *Research in Brief* 3, no. 1 (2021): https://www.acsi.org/docs/default-source/website-publishing/research/research-in-brief-fall-2021-final.pdf.

18. E.W. Carter, "A Place of Belonging: Research at the Intersection of Faith and Disability," *Review & Expositor* 113, no. 2 (2016): 168.

Chapter Four

1. By popular attribution.

2. R. Scott Rodin, 2010, *The Steward Leader: Transforming People, Organizations and Communities* (Downers Grove, IL: IVP Academic), 175.

3. EdChoice, "The ABCs of School Choice: The Comprehensive Guide to Every Private School Choice Program in America," 2022, https://www.edchoice.org/wp-content/uploads/2022/01/2022-ABCs-FINAL-WEB-002.pdf.

4. M.F. Lueken, "Fiscal Effects of School Choice: Analyzing the Costs and Savings of Private School Choice Programs in America," EdChoice, 2021, https://www.edchoice.org/wp-content/uploads/2021/11/The-Fiscal-Effects-of-School-Choice-WEB-reduced.pdf.

5. J.D. Reichard, "Religious Values and Tuition Vouchers: An Empirical Case Study of Parent Religiosity as a Factor of School Choice," *Journal of School Choice* 6, no. 4 (2012): 465–82.

6. C.E. Rouse, "Private School Vouchers and Student Achievement: An Evaluation of the Milwaukee Parental Choice Program," *The Quarterly Journal of Economics* 113, no. 2 (1998): 553–602.

7. J.P. Greene and R.H. Marsh, "The Effect of Milwaukee's Parental Choice Program on Student Achievement in Milwaukee Public Schools," SCDP Milwaukee Evaluation Report #11, 2009, University of Arkansas, https://eric.ed.gov/?id=ED530091.

8. R.M. Costrell, "The Fiscal Impact of the Milwaukee Parental Choice Program in Milwaukee and Wisconsin, 1993–2008," SCDP Milwaukee Evaluation Report #2, 2008, University of Arkansas, https://eric.ed.gov/?id=ED508632.

9. A. Berner, D. Bradford, and R. Pennings, "Making the Public-Good Case for Private Schools," Cardus, 2019, https://www.cardus.ca/wp-content/uploads/2019/10/2019-10-31_Making-the-the-Public-Good-Case-for-Private-Schools_Cardus.pdf.

10. C.A. DeAngelis, L.M. Burke, and P.J. Wolf, "The Effects of Regulations on Private School Choice Program Participation: Experimental Evidence from Florida," *Social Science Quarterly* 100, no. 6 (2019): 2316–36.

11. Lueken, "Fiscal Effects of School Choice."

12. In contrast, the aforementioned EdChoice program in Ohio features a copay prohibition, a common proviso in private school choice programs. A copay prohibition means that participating private schools must accept the value of the voucher as full payment of tuition, even if the cost of tuition exceeds the value of the voucher.

13. See Ohio Department of Education, "Fiscal Year 2022 Guidelines and Procedures for Auxiliary Services Program," October 2021, https://education.ohio.gov/getattachment/Topics/Ohio-Education-Options/Private-Schools/Nonpublic-Schools-Forms-and-Program-Information/FY22_Auxiliary-Service-Guidelines-1.pdf.aspx?lang=en-US.

14. L.E. Swaner and C. Marshall Powell, *Christian Schools and COVID-19: Responding Nimbly, Facing the Future* (Colorado Springs: Association of Christian Schools International, 2020).

15. P. Scott, "The Other Half of School Choice," *ACSI blog*, November 9, 2017, https://blog.acsi.org/christian-schools-parental-choice-programs.

Chapter Five

1. K. Robinson and L. Aronica, *Creative Schools: The Grassroots Revolution That's Transforming Education* (New York: Penguin, 2015), xxvi (emphases original).

2. R. Kegan and L. Laskow Lahey, *Immunity to Change: How to Overcome It and Unlock the Potential in Yourself and Your Organization* (Cambridge, MA: Harvard Business Review Press, 2009), 29.

3. T. Bolsinger, *Canoeing the Mountains: Christian Leadership in Unchartered Territory* (Downers Grove, IL: InterVarsity Press, 2015).

4. T. Elmore and A. McPeak, *Marching Off the Map: Inspire Students to Navigate a Brand New World* (Atlanta, GA: Poet Gardener Publishing, 2017).

5. L.E. Swaner, D. Beerens, and E. Ellefsen, eds., *MindShift: Catalyzing Change in Christian Education* (Colorado Springs: Association of Christian Schools International, 2019).

6. Robinson and Aronica, *Creative Schools*, xx–xxii.

7. F. Vermeulen and N. Sivanathan, "Stop Doubling Down on Your Failing Strategy," *Harvard Business Review*, November-December 2017, https://hbr.org/2017/11/stop-doubling-down-on-your-failing-strategy.

8. ACSI, "2020–2021 Tuition & Salary Survey Member Report," Association of Christian Schools International, 2021.

9. L.E. Swaner and M.H. Lee, *Christian Schools and COVID-19: 2020–2021 School Year Profile* (Colorado Springs: Association of Christian Schools International, 2020).

10. A. Wolfman-Arent, "New Pa. Data Shows How the Pandemic Gave a Big Boost to Cyber Charter Schools," WHYY PBS/NPR, December 8, 2020, https://whyy.org/articles/new-pa-data-shows-how-the-pandemic-gave-a-big-boost-to-cyber-charter-schools/.

11. J.K. Cavanaugh, "Are Online Courses Cannibalizing Students from Existing Courses?," *Online Learning* 9, no. 3 (2019): http://dx.doi.org/10.24059/olj.v9i3.1781.

12. T. Vander Ark and L. Dobyns, *Better Together: How to Leverage School Networks for Smarter Personalized and Project Based Learning* (San Francisco: Jossey-Bass, 2018), 6–7, 14.

13. M. McShane, "School Choice Keeps Winning," *Forbes*, June 12, 2021, https://www.forbes.com/sites/mikemcshane/2021/07/12/school-choice-keeps-winning.

14. E. Wearne and J. Thompson, *National Hybrid Schools Survey 2022* (Kennesaw, GA: Kennesaw State University Coles College of Business, 2022).

15. Robinson and Aronica, *Creative Schools*, xxiii.

Chapter Six

1. C. Heath and D. Heath, *The Power of Moments: Why Certain Experiences Have Extraordinary Impact* (New York: Simon & Schuster, 2017), 131.

2. J. Eckert, *The Novice Advantage: Fearless Practice for Every Teacher* (Thousand Oaks, CA: Corwin, 2016).

3. A.M. Grant, *Originals: How Non-conformists Move the World* (New York: Viking, 2016).

4. R.A. Heifetz, *Leadership Without Easy Answers* (Cambridge, MA: Harvard University Press, 1994).

5. A. De Smet, "Your Organization Is Grieving—Here's How You Can Help," *McKinsey Quarterly*, September 17, 2020, https://www.mckinsey.com/business-functions/people-and-organizational-performance/our-insights/your-organization-is-grieving-heres-how-you-can-help.

6. R. Evans, *The Human Side of Change: Reform, Resistance, and the Real-Life Problems of Innovation* (San Francisco: Jossey-Bass, 1996), 28–29.

Chapter Seven

1. R. Stearns, *Lead Like It Matters to God: Values-Driven Leadership in a Success-Driven World* (Downers Grove, IL: InterVarsity Press, 2021), 18.

2. E. Hanushek, "The Trade-Off Between Child Quantity and Quality," *Journal of Political Economy* 100, no. 1 (1992): 84–117; S.G. Rivkin, E.A. Hanushek, and J.F. Kain, "Teachers, Schools, and Academic Achievement," *Econometrica* 73, no. 2 (2005): 417–58; W.L. Sanders and J.C. Rivers, "Cumulative and Residual Effects of Teachers on Future Student Academic Achievement: Research Progress Report," University of Tennessee Value-Added Research and Assessment Center, 1996.

3. D.E. DeMatthews, S. Kotok, and A. Serafini, "Leadership Preparation for Special Education and Inclusive Schools: Beliefs and Recommendations from Successful Principals," *Journal of Research on Leadership Education* 15, no. 4 (2020): 303–29; M. Lee, J.H. Ryoo, and A. Walker, "School Principals' Time Use for Interaction with Individual Students: Macro Contexts, Organizational Conditions, and Student Outcomes," *American Journal of Education* 127, no. 2 (2021): 303–44; K.S. Louis, K Leithwood, W.L. Wahlstrom, and S.E. Anderson, "Investigating the Links to Improved Student Learning: Final Report of Research Findings," The Wallace Foundation, July 2010, http://www.wallacefoundation.org/knowledge-center/Documents/Investigating-the-Links-to-Improved-Student-Learning.pdf; T. Waters, R.J. Marzano, and B. McNulty, "Balanced Leadership: What 30 Years of Research Tells Us About the Effect of Leadership on Student Achievement," Mid-Continent Research for Education and Learning, 2003.

4. T. Calik, F. Sezgin, H. Kavagaci, and A. Kilinc, "Relationships Between Instructional Leadership of School Principals and Self-Efficacy of Teachers and Collective Teacher Efficacy," *Educational Sciences: Theory & Practice* 12, no. 4 (2012): 2498–2504.

5. L. Swaner, C.A. Marshall, and S.A. Tesar, *Flourishing Schools: Research on Christian School Culture and Community* (Colorado Springs: Association of Christian Schools International, 2019).

6. M. Will, "Teachers Are Not OK, Even Though We Need Them to Be," *EdWeek*, September 14, 2021, https://www.edweek.org/teaching-learning/teachers-are-not-ok-even-though-we-need-them-to-be/2021/09; T. Walker, "Educators Ready for Fall, but a Teacher Shortage Looms," *National Education Association (NEA) News*, June 17, 2021, https://www.nea.org/advocating-for-change/new-from-nea/educators-ready-fall-teacher-shortage-looms.

7. *National Association of Secondary School Principals Bulletin*, "NASSP Survey Signals a Looming Mass Exodus of Principals from Schools," December 8, 2021, https://www.nassp.org/news/nassp-survey-signals-a-looming-mass-exodus-of-principals-from-schools/.

8. L.E. Swaner, C. Dodds, and M.H. Lee, *Leadership for Flourishing Schools: From Research to Practice* (Colorado Springs: Association of Christian Schools International, 2021).

9. L.E. Swaner and J. Ferguson, "Christian School Leadership: 2019 ACSI profile," *ACSI blog*, February 4, 2020, https://blog.acsi.org/christian-school-leadership-2019-acsi-profile; M.H. Lee, A. Cheng, and K. Wiens, "2020 Principal Survey," Council on Educational Standards & Accountability, 2021, https://www.cesaschools.org/assets/docs/cesa-survey-final-final1.pdf.

10. Stearns, *Lead Like It Matters to God*, 18.

11. L.E. Swaner and C. Marshall Powell, *Christian Schools and COVID-19: Responding Nimbly, Facing the Future* (Colorado Springs: Association of Christian Schools International, 2020).

12. P.J. Palmer, *The Courage to Teach: Exploring the Inner Landscape of a Teacher's Life* (San Francisco: Jossey-Bass, 1998), 3.

13. Palmer, *Courage to Teach*, 3.

Chapter Eight

1. John 1:14 according to The Message, quoted in D. Pampuch and D. Iselin, "From Siloed to Engaged," in *MindShift: Catalyzing Christian Education*, ed. L.E. Swaner, D. Beerens, and E. Ellefsen (Colorado Springs: Association of Christian Schools International, 2019), 93–106 (quote on 103).

2. L. Kyriakides, B. Creemers, P. Antoniou, and D. Demetrious, "A Synthesis of Studies Searching for School Factors: Implications for Theory and Research," *British Educational Research Journal* 36, no. 5 (2010): 807–30.

3. L. Swaner, C.A. Marshall, and S.A. Tesar, *Flourishing Schools: Research on Christian School Culture and Community* (Colorado Springs: Association of Christian Schools International, 2019).

4. Pampuch and Iselin, "From Siloed to Engaged," 96.

5. K. Chenoweth, "How Do We Get There from Here?," *Educational Leadership* 72, no. 5 (2015): 16–20; D. Hopkins and D. Reynolds, "The Past, Present, and Future of School Improvement: Towards the Third Age," *British Educational Research Journal* 27,

no. 4 (2001): 459–75; A. Bryk, "Organizing Schools for Improvement," *The Phi Delta Kappan* 91, no. 7 (2010): 23–30.

6. We use the term "families" in this chapter instead of "parents" in recognition that sometimes adults other than biological or adoptive parents fulfill the parenting role for students (e.g., grandparents, legal guardians).

7. S. D. Horsford and T. Holmes-Sutton, "Parent and Family Engagement: The Missing Piece in Urban Education Reform," *The Lincy Institute Policy Brief* 2 (2012): https://digitalscholarship.unlv.edu/lincy_publications/15/; J. Smith, P. Wohlstetter, C. Ally Kuzin, and K. De Pedro, "Parent Involvement in Urban Charter Schools: New Strategies for Increasing Participation," *The School Community Journal* 21, no. 1 (2011): 71–94.

8. See https://www.talberthouse.org/about/ for more about Talbert House.

9. See https://www.siskin.org/5/about-us for more on Siskin Children's Institute.

Chapter Nine

1. P. Greer, C. Horst, and J. Heisey, *Rooting for Rivals: How Collaboration and Generosity Increase the Impact of Leaders, Charities, and Churches* (Bloomington, MN: Bethany House, 2018), 19.

2. L. Dahlander and M. Wallin, "Why Now Is the Time for 'Open Innovation,'" *Harvard Business Review*, June 5, 2020, https://hbr.org/2020/06/why-now-is-the-time-for-open-innovation.

3. Greer, Horst, and Heisey, *Rooting for Rivals*, 19.

4. E. Wenger, "Communities of Practice and Social Learning Systems," *Organization* 7, no. 2 (2000): 225–46.

5. R. DuFour and R. Eaker, *Professional Learning Communities at Work: Best Practices for Enhancing Student Achievement* (Bloomington, IN: Solution Tree Press, 1998).

6. A.S. Bryk, L.M. Gomez, A. Grunow, and P.G. LeMahieu, *Learning to Improve: How America's Schools Can Get Better at Getting Better* (Cambridge, MA: Harvard Education Press, 2015).

7. A. Grant, *Think Again: The Power of Knowing What You Don't Know* (New York: Viking Press, 2021).

8. P. Greer, C. Horst, and A. Haggard, *Mission Drift: The Unspoken Crisis Facing Leaders, Charities, and Churches* Minneapolis: Bethany House, 2014).

9. Greer, Horst, and Heisey, *Rooting for Rivals*, 22.

10. L. Swaner, C.A. Marshall, and S.A. Tesar, *Flourishing Schools: Research on Christian School Culture and Community* (Colorado Springs: Association of Christian Schools International, 2019).

11. Greer, Horst, and Heisey, *Rooting for Rivals*, 20–21.

Epilogue

1. T. Elmore and A. McPeak, *Marching Off the Map: Inspire Students to Navigate a Brand New World* (Atlanta, GA: Poet Gardener Publishing, 2017)

2. T. Bolsinger, *Canoeing the Mountains: Christian Leadership in Unchartered Territory* (Downers Grove, IL: InterVarsity Press, 2015).

3. J.K.A. Smith, *You Are What You Love: The Spiritual Power of Habit* (Grand Rapids: Brazos, 2016).

ABOUT THE AUTHORS

Lynn E. Swaner, EdD, is the chief strategy and innovation officer at Association of Christian Schools International, where she leads initiatives and develops strategies to address compelling questions and challenges facing Christian education. Dr. Swaner serves as a Cardus senior fellow and is the co-author or editor of numerous books on Christian education, including *Flourishing Together: A Christian Vision for Students, Educators, and Schools* and *MindShift: Catalyzing Change in Christian Education*. Prior to joining ACSI, she served as a professor of education and a Christian school administrator in New York. She holds an EdD in organization and leadership from Teachers College, Columbia University.

Jon Eckert, EdD, is the Copple Professor for Christians in School Leadership at Baylor University and a Cardus senior fellow. He taught intermediate and middle school students outside Chicago and Nashville for twelve years. He completed his doctorate at Vanderbilt University and served at the US Department of Education during the Bush and Obama administrations. For ten years, he prepared teachers at Wheaton College. He is the author of *The Novice Advantage: Fearless Practice for Every Teacher* and *Leading Together: Teachers and Administrators Improving Student Outcomes*, as well as numerous book chapters and articles. He researches collective leadership, teaching quality, and school improvement through the Baylor Center for School Leadership.

Erik Ellefsen is Director of Network and Improvement at Baylor University's Center for School Leadership. He has served in education for more than two decades as a teacher, coach, consultant, and as dean of academics at Boston Trinity Academy, principal at Chicago Christian High School, and grievance chairman for the American Federation of Teachers. He currently serves as senior fellow for both the Center for the Advancement of Christian Education and Cardus. He is a graduate of Wheaton College, with a BA in social science and Illinois teacher accreditation and an MEd in administration and leadership from Benedictine University with Illinois administrative credential, and he attended Boston University to further his studies in educational policy and organizational leadership.

Matthew H. Lee, PhD, is director of research at the Association of Christian Schools International and an adjunct professor of education policy at Johns Hopkins University, where he teaches a course on education finance. He is co-editor of *Religious Liberty and Education* (Rowman & Littlefield, 2020) and author of numerous peer-reviewed research articles, book chapters, technical reports, and op-eds on civics education, education leadership, and religious education. He previously taught history at a public charter school in Massachusetts. He holds a BA in political science from Davidson College and a PhD in education policy from the University of Arkansas.

About the Association of Christian Schools International (ACSI)

ACSI is the world's largest Protestant school association, with close to 5,500 member schools in over 100 countries including the United States and Canada. ACSI's mission is to strengthen Christian schools and equip Christian educators worldwide as they prepare students academically and inspire students to become devoted followers of Jesus Christ.

About Cardus

Cardus is a non-partisan think tank dedicated to clarifying and strengthening, through research and dialogue, the ways in which society's institutions can work together for the common good.

About Cardus Education

Cardus Education exists to cultivate education for the common good and convene education leaders, through original research and policy studies on educational pluralism, excellence in education, and graduate outcomes.